Survivors of War

*One Family's Struggle
Through World War II*

*Based on the memories of
Walerian Joseph Dobrucki*

Dan Dobrucki

Survivors of War, One Family's Struggle Through World War II

Based on the memories of Walerian Joseph Dobrucki

Copyright ©2011 – Dan Dobrucki

All rights reserved, including but not limited to reproduction in whole or in part in any media form, including and form of storage retrieval system, without the written permission of publisher.

ISBN: 978-0-578-06548-9

Library of Congress Cataloging-in-Publication

Printed in the United States of America

On the Front Cover: Walerian Joseph Dobrucki circa.1939

On the Back Cover: The Family in Wellandport, September, 2011
Back Row: Dan Dobrucki, Walerian Joseph Dobrucki, Rick Dobrucki
Middle Row: Joe Dobrucki, Angie Greenwood, Sarayah Killins, Kim
              Killins, Alexis Killins
Front Row: Ella Dobrucki, Kaeli Killins, Ty Greenwood, Meg Greenwood

Crestview Press books are available for business, education and promotional discounts. For information, please contact marketing at: marketing@crestviewpress.com, or by mail: 3571 E. Sunset Road, Las Vegas, NV 89120

CRESTVIEW PRESS

Dedicated to the memory of my brother Gary

Of all the death that I witnessed in war,
nothing prepared me for the pain and
devastation of losing my son Gary,
in a reckless car accident.

Walerian Joseph Dobrucki

Table of Contents

Introduction	7
Chapter 1 – February 10, 1940	23
Chapter 2 – The First Year-Spring 1940	35
Chapter 3 – Winter, 1940-41	67
Chapter 4 – Another Year-Early 1941	79
Chapter 5 – May 1941 – Bricks	89
Chapter 6 – September 1941	95
Chapter 7 – Spring, 1942	113
Chapter 8 – Back To The War	123
Chapter 9 – Decisions	135
Conclusion	145
Appendix	151

Copyright ©2011 – Dan Dobrucki

Introduction

It was the 1st of September 1939 and the world was poised for war. The Germans, who had been embarrassed by their loss in World War I — the "War To End All Wars", were spoiling for vengeance.

The Russians were eager to spread their Communist Revolution. They had also been embarrassed in previous wars. After World War I — the "War To End All Wars" they had lost their western territories from which an independent Poland and Baltic nations had been recreated.

The Russians, in 1918, attacked Poland. They used their entire military might to try and restore their empire. They met a humiliating defeat by a much smaller army.

The French were tired of war. A large part of the World War I was fought on French soil. The French seemed afraid of another war. In Britain, Neville Chamberlain gave up Czechoslovakia rather than confront Hitler. The British seemed to feel that they had stopped any further aggression.

Americans were happy in their corner of the world. As long as the other powers stayed away from the Western Hemisphere, Americans didn't care what was happening in the rest of the world.

Hitler and Stalin, unbeknownst to us, had already made an alliance. They had already agreed to invade Poland and had even agreed how to split the country between themselves.

Our (Poland's) allies were the British and the French. They guaranteed that they would maintain our borders. Poland was not allowed to modernize our armed forces because that might be a provocation to Germany and might lead to war. Most of our weapons dated back to our last war against Russia. Even as war was imminent, Poland was told not to call up her reservists.

On September 1st, Hitler invaded in what he called a pre-emptive war. War, he stated, was necessary to protect Germany. I was a 23-year-old corporal, ready to finish my army service, when we were invaded. I was part of a supply unit in charge of 11 wagons that were loaded with supplies for our forces. We carried everything from grenades to saddles and had several anti tank cannons for protection.

We were far from the German front when the war began. It wasn't until days later that we saw our first German. It was in the form of a Stuka dive-bomber. As we were moving our wagons forward, he attacked. The

Stukas were equipped with a siren that produced a load, hideous scream as they dove. The horses were so scared that we couldn't control them.

Fortunately, as the Stuka dived, my team headed for the forest and safety.

We had no radios and we didn't know where we were supposed to go. Our orders would have to come by messenger. So we waited.

The orders came in the form of a cavalry unit. An officer rode up to us, "The Germans are breaking through. We're reforming across the Vistula River to protect Warsaw. Leave your wagons, take your artillery and follow us."

We all knew that we had to hold out. The British and the French had declared war against Germany. But they were still sitting along their borders, sending messages to Hitler. The French government said that it would take two weeks before they could attack in full force. We had to hold the Germans until the 14th of September.

I grabbed a saddle, from the supply wagon, and threw it on one of my horses. I chose our largest horse, a white stallion. And we were off — almost.

The horse was used to pulling heavy loads but wasn't used to being ridden. He took a few tentative steps and stopped. I hit him but he wouldn't move. So, I gave him my spurs. He took off at a trot for a few hundred yards and stopped. I was already well behind my entire unit, except for one other private. He was also having trouble with his horse.

He was on the ground, holding on to the reins as the horse reared up on its hind legs. It was a much smaller horse than mine; black, spirited, obviously an officer's horse.

"I can't handle this horse." He cried out.

I was used to horses so I made him an offer. "Let's trade horses."

He was agreeable as long as he could keep his saddle. After a few minutes, I was off again. This horse knew how to run.

Somewhere ahead of us (ahead of the horse and me) I heard artillery fire. There was a battle taking place. I headed towards the sound. I saw smoke in the field. A German tank had been destroyed and was smoking. As we got closer, a German soldier popped out of the tank. Before I could react, POP, a gunshot in the distance. The soldier slumped, a bullet hole in the middle of his head.

I couldn't find anyone so we moved on.

Further along was another German tank. We had trees, in Poland, which we cut for firewood. When the trees were cut, several sprouts would grow from the stump. We would cut these sprouts and more would grow. The size, of the stump, would keep increasing. It would be large and sturdy but the sprouts would make it look like a small bush. A German tank driver, believing that it was a bush, drove into it. His tank was upside down; totally destroyed.

There was another disabled tank not far away. An artillery shell had taken out its track. I was obviously behind the German lines.

We followed the tracks of the cavalry through the forests but we were well behind. At night, I let my horse follow the trail. He seemed able to follow the scent of the other horses. That night I slept on my horse as we kept traveling.

As dawn broke, I awoke having no idea where I was. To one side, there was a farm. I turned my horse towards it. There was no one to be seen. I called out but there was no answer. I hadn't eaten since yesterday noon so I decided to stop.

The important things had to be done first so I went to the well and drew out some water. My horse needed to drink. Then I found him some grain. Only after he was cared for, I entered the house. There was a fire burning, the kerosene lamp was lit and a bag of flour lay on the table. But no one was home. Obviously, they had just fled.

I made pancakes for my breakfast. I ate as much as I could and packed the rest into my knapsack.

We continued east, towards the Vistula River. I hadn't seen a single person since that German in the tank. There was less forest now along the road I was traveling. That's when I heard a buzzing noise, in the sky, behind me. It was a German plane.

I had been caught out in the open. There was a small clump of trees a few hundred yards from me. I decided to race for it just as the pilot decided to go for me. There were not enough trees in which to hide but there was one very large tree. I headed for it.

The plane behind me was a Messerschmitt, not the Stuka dive-bomber. The pilot opened fire but I was already behind the tree. I dismounted and kept the tree between the plane and myself and the horse. The bullets just went past us. My horse must have been well trained. He stood still as the plane flew over us.

The plane turned and came at us again. We moved to the other side of the tree. The bullets, again, passed harmlessly past us. A few more passes and the plane flew off.

We continued east. That evening, I found another farm to stop at. The buildings were hidden inside a large fence. Once again, I called out without getting a response. The place was deserted. I quickly found food and water for my horse. That was a priority. And then I found a pleasant surprise.

Our army had to have been here, and not that long ago. They had left behind a kitchen on wheels. It was an entire kitchen, stove, fuel and all the ingredients for a good meal placed on a wagon, so that men could get good food regardless of where they were.

I made myself fresh coffee and filled a canteen. I cooked some ham and placed it between 2 of my pancakes. I had a hot meal as I left the farmhouse behind. The Vistula couldn't be too far away.

That night I found a forested area to stay. I took the saddle from my horse and, using it as a pillow, went to sleep. I tied the horse to a bush, leaving enough rope to let him graze as much as he wanted.

It was still dark when I was awakened by horses galloping past me. "We've opened the road to Warsaw." Someone called out from the darkness. "Hurry, before the Germans counter attack."

These were the first people I had seen in days, even though I hadn't actually seen anyone. Again we were off towards Warsaw.

Now, suddenly, there were hundreds of soldiers, as well as thousands of civilians, along the road. All of them were headed for Warsaw to make one last stand against the Germans.

The road was rough. It had been under construction. Large stones were placed on the road but it hadn't been paved. I didn't slow down, which was probably a mistake.

My horse cried out, stopped and went down to his knees. I dismounted and tried to get him back up to no avail. He had broken his shoe and cut his hoof. There wasn't much I could do. My father was a blacksmith so I had always worked with horses. I knew what had to be done. I took out my knife and, carefully, removed what was left of his shoe. If I tried riding him anymore, the leg could only get worse. I bandaged his leg and we began walking.

In the distance, I saw a barn, with a corral, and headed for it. Once again, the farm was deserted but I did find three horses in the corral. Two were workhorses but the third one had promise. He was a good-looking three-year-old. I put my bridle on him and he stood still. I took the saddle off my horse and put it on the three-year-old. He stood still.

I got on. He was obviously used to being ridden.

I left my horse behind, as a trade, and continued towards Warsaw.

Warsaw was now congested with people, all its residents, the refugees and 100,000 soldiers defending their capitol. As long as Warsaw held out, Poland was not defeated. We had to hold out until our allies could attack Germany along their western borders.

Once inside Warsaw, I needed to find a place to stay and a unit to join. I found Lazienkowski Park where military units were forming. One unit had artillery pieces that looked just like those of my unit so that was where I headed. To my astonishment, this was my unit. They had arrived only hours before I did.

I reported for duty.

We still didn't have any radios to communicate with other units. I was going to be a messenger and scout. My first assignment was to check an area, at the edge of the city, that we were about to shell. The Germans were entering Warsaw and the Polish forces needed the artillery to help stop them.

By the time I reached the area, it had already fallen to the Germans.

This is what I did for the next few weeks. I checked our lines to see where the enemy was. I carried messages back and forth. Whether on horseback, on foot, on the street, the alleys or moving through the sewers.

The Germans kept pounding us. The capture of Warsaw was taking longer than expected. Shortly after we were surrounded, Hitler had come to the outskirts of Warsaw hoping to see it fall and enter as conqueror. He left in a rage.

Their artillery kept shelling us. Day and night, their planes dropped bombs on us. The shelling and bombing were so constant that we stopped taking cover when planes came over the city. Bombers were always over the city.

With every plane, more people died, and not just the soldiers. They didn't aim at us only. They wanted to punish the city.

But we had held out. Two weeks had passed and now, we were certain, our French and British allies were ready to invade Germany. Most of the best German military units were fighting us so their western borders were lightly defended. It would be easy to march through them, straight to Berlin.

We waited. Sept. 14th. Nothing happened.

Sept. 15th. Nothing.

Sept. 16th. Still nothing.

Sept. 17th. The invasion came. But not the one we were hoping for. Stalin, Hitler's ally, finally understood that the British and French were going to remain, sitting, on their collective asses. He attacked our eastern borders where we had almost no troops to stop him. Not that it mattered to the Russian troops. They were going to kill anyone in their way just for the fun of it. In reality, the war was over. But we kept holding out, hoping for a miracle.

The bombings continued.

It was on one of these bombing runs, no different than thousands of other bombing runs, that the bombs hit our unit. Some of our men lay dead; others were wounded. A piece of shrapnel tore into my leg. It wasn't a life-threatening wound but it was enough to take me out of the battle.

A doctor cleaned the wound, wrapped my leg, found me a set of crutches and put me to the side.

We were the wounded, trying to take care of ourselves and keep out of the way of the fighting. I took my horse and two draught horses and took care of them. They needed to be fed and watered just as much as we did.

Then one day a man came up to me while I was tending these horses. "I'd like to buy your draught horses." He said.

"Well, they're not mine. They belong to the army." I informed him.

It didn't seem to make any difference. He explained that Warsaw was about to fall. And then the Germans would take the horses.

"I'll give you 1,500 Zloty for the two of them," he offered.

I thought over his proposal. They weren't my horses so I didn't feel right taking so much money from this man. But I felt that, somehow, I would need the money. So I said, "give me 1,000 Zloty and take the horses."

The next day, the same man came back to me. "I'll give you another 1,000 Zloty for your last horse."

"You can have him for 500 Zloty."

As the Germans kept attacking, we kept moving. Yet, somehow, this same man found me. "I need some wagons and some more horses. If you can find them, I'll pay you." I now knew the area. I found a wagon that was in good condition. Then I found some horses that were still alive. And each time, that I did, this same man found me. True to his word, he paid me each time. I eventually had 5,500 Zloty stuffed in my boot. I never found out who he was or what became of him.

Warsaw was now in ruins. There were fires everywhere. Smoke mingled with the dust to produce a constant haze in the city. Some people, who knew the area, managed to slip out through the forests around Warsaw. Most of us didn't know the area and were trapped. Thousands of soldiers would eventually reach France in hopes of continuing our fight against Germany.

On Sept. 28, Warsaw surrendered. Poland was, again, defeated. In this prelude to the new world war, over 16,000 German soldiers were killed. 20% of the planes and 25% of the tanks, used to attack us, were destroyed. Our casualties were much larger. We fought to give our allies time to attack Germany. It was a waste of good lives.

I was now a prisoner. The Germans offered to take me to a medical unit but I said "No". I would march, even on crutches, with the other soldiers.

There were tens of thousands of men marched out of Warsaw. It was hard marching and I ended up near the back of the line. As darkness fell, we continued marching. We came along side a deep ditch and I motioned to a friend, who was helping me walk. Together, we slipped into the ditch unseen by our guards.

Now we would have to find our way back home. It was going to be difficult. Not only was I still on crutches but also there were Germans everywhere. And we were escaped prisoners of war.

We began meeting other Polish soldiers. They had been captured and processed. They were given papers that allowed them to travel through German occupied Poland and go home.

This seemed a better way of getting home than our original plan. At the next town we reached, we surrendered again. We were processed but weren't released. We would have to stay at a prisoner of war camp.

The conditions weren't good — the Germans didn't really care about their enemies — and we were always hungry. I knew enough German to get by and began talking with one of the guards. It didn't take long to talk him into letting me go to town. After all, "How far can I get on these crutches?" I asked him.

Once in town, I arranged to have several vats of soup delivered to the prison. I also bought a small bottle of Schnapps for the guard who let me out. From now on, I had no trouble getting out to buy more food.

I just needed to find this guard. All I had to do was bring him a bottle when I came back.

But we still weren't released. Instead, all the remaining prisoners were going to be marched to a new P.O.W. camp. My leg still wasn't ready for a long march. I talked to the German in charge. He allowed me to take a horse and ride during the march.

There were thousands of prisoners, hundreds of guards all on foot. And there I was, the only person riding.

The new camp wasn't anything formal. There were tents set in a large field. Guards walked around the camp but there was no major fencing to keep us in. Once again, I started talking to the guards. I found one who was a Slovak. I knew how to speak Slovakian so I began talking with him regularly and talked him into letting me out to go to town. I used the same line on him as the other guard. "How far can I get on these crutches?"

There were probably about 10,000 prisoners in this camp. I couldn't buy enough food for everyone, so I bought food for the men in my tent.

I would go to town on a regular basis. On one trip, I approached a young man who appeared to be a student. After telling him my story, I gave him some money. "Please find me a good compass and a map of this region. And keep them, for me, until I need them."

Each time I returned, I brought back a bottle for my Slovak guard.

Eventually, I traded in my crutches for a cane. But I was still allowed out. After all, I did come back every evening. There was no reason to try to escape. Not until the Germans started bringing in truckloads of tall posts and barbed wire.

There were 7 men, in my tent, that I trusted completely. I went to them with a plan. The next morning, we all picked up pails and went to see the guard.

"We're going out to buy some food." I explained.

The Slovak guard thought it over for a moment and let all of us out. Once we were out of sight, we dropped the pails and went to find the young man who, I hoped, would have my compass and map. He did. We then headed east.

This was going to be a real prison soon and this may have been our last chance to escape. Now we headed for the new German - Russian border. All of us had homes on the Russian side.

We traveled through the countryside, avoiding the populated areas. Each night, we would find a farmhouse and ask for food and a place to sleep. We were never turned away. We were never betrayed. And, when we left, I always left behind a few Zloty.

We arrived at a river that was the new border. I asked the farmer, with whose family we had spent the night, if he thought we would be able to safely cross the river.

The bridges were still intact. That wouldn't be a problem. And it wasn't heavily patrolled on either side. The patrols didn't occur on a regular basis so we would have to take a chance if we wanted to get across. When we reached the bridge, there were no signs of soldiers on either side. We had no choice. We crossed.

Just before we made it to the other side, a number of Russian trucks roared around the corner. We were caught on the edge of the bridge with nowhere to hide.

A soldier jumped from a truck, demanding to know who we were and what we were doing.

"The Germans had taken us prisoner." I explained in Russian. "They are releasing their prisoners. We're heading south on our way home."

And I showed him the papers the Germans had given me. He studied them for several minutes. But there was nothing, on these papers, that said we had been released. He ordered us onto a truck and we were off. We stopped in a town square filled with people and were ordered out.

"There's the train station." The soldier volunteered. "It'll take you south."

Fortunately, he couldn't read German. He had no idea we were escaped P.O.W.s.

I bought tickets for all of us and we were on our way home.

There were problems in our home area after the Russian invasion. Over the centuries, Poland had been partitioned among the Russian, Austrian and German empires. These empires would bring their own citizens into the occupied territories to rule a conquered people.

The largest city, in my home area, was Lwow. There were mostly Poles living in this area as well as some Ukrainians and a few Russians. Now the Russians and Ukrainians had power and they wanted to cement their control. We were warned to be careful of any mobs.

I lived the furthest south, in the village of Stefanufka near Kalusz, so I was the last, of our group, to get off the train. The station was packed. I was worried as I left the train. The crowd, seeing me in uniform, flocked towards me.

"Where did you come from? How did you get home? Are our sons coming?"

I didn't have any real news for them and didn't want to stay here any longer than necessary. I told them what they wanted to hear. I said that I had been released. Other prisoners would, eventually, be released and they would be on their way.

Finally, I was home.

Chapter One – February 10, 1940

The dogs were the first to sense the danger on that calm, moonlit night when the Russians came for us.

They started barking when the troops were still far away. It was only 5 o'clock and all the windows were covered with ice. By the time I had dressed and reached the door, to look outside, horse drawn sleighs were entering our village.

I was ready for this. The Russians had been searching all of conquered Poland, looking for soldiers who had evaded capture, and I was a soldier.

One of the sleighs stopped in front of our house. Four soldiers got out and approached the gate where they stopped. They had been met by our 3 German Shepherds and didn't dare enter our yard.

"Get these dogs away from here." They began yelling. "Open this gate and let us in."

Father called back to them, as he got dressed. He went out slowly and pulled the dogs away. This gave me time to put on my uniform and grab a parcel of food that I had prepared in case of exactly this type of problem.

From the back door the forest was only 40 meters away. While Father was keeping the soldiers busy, I ran out the back and into the woods. There, I hid and watched what was happening at the house.

It was 10 to 15 minutes before I heard screaming then crying coming from the house. I left the parcel and ran back. When I came running in, a Russian, holding a gun turned to me and yelled "Rieki-w-wierch!" ("hands up").

After searching me, he holstered his gun. Then he told us to get dressed because we were going to be moved. This area was to be declared a military zone and everyone, from the village, was being evacuated. There would be no other choice.

I spoke some Russian so I began talking with the officer. He kept saying that we were being taken from our village but he wouldn't tell us where we were being taken. I had two silver bars on my uniform so the Russian mistook me for an officer and treated me as a military equal. His uniform had similar bars made of nickel but, whereas he was a lieutenant, I was still only a corporal.

His mannerisms made me feel that he was ashamed of what he was doing. I told him that I couldn't believe that they were removing everyone.

"If we are the only ones to be taken away, we won't leave this village. You may as well kill us all where we stand." I said. "It is a soldier's duty to protect civilians; not to kill them."

Finally, I convinced him to let me check my uncle, who lived three houses down, and a few neighbors. He came with me and I saw that, at every house, there was a Russian soldier with three armed Ukrainian civilians herding the people between their homes and the sleighs.

My uncle spoke perfect Russian and had been listening to the soldiers talking. "I have no doubt. They are taking us to Siberia." He told me.

When I came back home, we were told to put on as many layers of clothing as we could. "Whatever you have on, you will be able to keep." We were told. "I have no idea what will happen with anything that you leave behind."

I put on as many of my civilian clothes as I could under my uniform. I wore my boots and put extra pairs of shoes into my pockets. Everyone in the family did the same as did everyone else in the entire village.

There was one sleigh in front of each house. Each sleigh would transport that family and whatever goods they were able to load into it.

We took bed sheets and wrapped them around our pillows and blankets. We emptied a large chest and filled it with 100 kilos of meat and fat from a pig we had butchered the day before. Mother stuffed six loaves of bread and other food into the chest until it was full. This would keep us alive for the next few weeks during our transport and the first days in Siberia.

Mother wanted to take her sewing machine but the Ukrainians wouldn't allow it. No doubt, they thought that maybe they would be able to "liberate" it for themselves. We added a bag of flour onto the sleigh and climbed in.

Left behind was 500 kilos of flour, 100 kilos of honey, our grain, all the produce we had harvested and all our belongings that we weren't allowed to take with us. Our cows and pigs were left in the barn; unmilked and unfed.

Then, quickly, they took us to the local factory railway station. There we waited all day and into the night. It was late that night when a train, pulling cattle cars, arrived. We were loaded into these cars and taken to the main railway station at Kalusz.

We were unloaded into a crowd of thousands of people who were already there. Beyond the station, in the fields, the Russians were piling the crops that they were confiscating from our farms. Stacks of grain, of beets, of potatoes and other crops were left uncovered and unprotected from the elements to freeze and rot.

Again, we waited all day for another train to come. That evening, they loaded us into more cattle cars and took us to Lwow.

At Lwow, there were already tens of thousands of people waiting. Others would follow us. Everywhere you looked, there were people dressed in too many clothes trying to hold onto whatever possessions they still had. Soldiers and armed civilians kept them in check.

The Russian train tracks were wider than other European tracks so none of our trains could move into mother Russia. Therefore, the Russians built a train track into Lwow. This became one of the centers for the deportation of millions of Polish people.

That evening, trains began arriving pulling special Russian "Pullman" cargo cars, which were just cattle cars and freight cars, converted to carrying people. We were told to leave all our belongings and get into these cars. No one moved. As the soldiers began pushing people, the people pushed back.

They began yelling. Some yelled, in Russian, to the soldiers or, in Ukrainian, to the armed civilians. "We're not getting into these cars. Not without the few things, in this world, that we have left."

This could have easily turned into a riot until an officer took over and told the rail workers to bring in extra cars. These cars were added onto each train and we were allowed to store our belongings in them. Then we began boarding.

"Every family take some water with you. You're going to need it." We were told.

Father took two pails of water. Other than that, we were only allowed to take blankets and pillows aboard with us.

"You are not prisoners." We were told. "You are "specjalne

przeciedlency" (special guests) of the Soviet Empire. You are being relocated to the Communist "Heaven", the worker's "paradise"."

Each train pulled a number of 16 tonne cars into which they put 30-40 people and 35 tonne cars that would hold 70-80 people. Along the walls of each car, boards were hung to make berths on which people could sit. Other people had to sit on the floor, below the berths. In the middle, of each car, there was a small stove with a pile of wood or occasionally some coal. Behind the stove, a small hole was cut. This was going to be our toilet for the duration of our trip. The hole was too small to allow even a child to escape but it was big enough to freeze everything inside once the train started moving.

They closed the doors and bolted them shut. Each car had only two small windows. Not that it mattered much because we would be moved mostly at night. During the day, if there were a town ahead, we would be stopped. It seemed that they wanted to keep something secret. Either they didn't want anyone to see us or they didn't want us to see what was outside.

There was still some light out when we crossed the Polish Russian border and finally saw this Russian heaven. The border town, on the Polish side, was Woloczyska and on the Russian side was Pod-Woloczyska. It was one town divided by a barbed wire fence with guard towers on the Russian side. The Polish half was a normal, prosperous farming town with good houses and well-kept barns. On the Russian side, the houses were drab, not well looked after and there seemed to be no barns. There were horses and sheep roaming the streets and standing against the houses.

The land was identical on both sides of the border. The people had also been the same for generations. But then Stalin came into power in Soviet Russia.

Stalin ordered all farms to be taken from the people and made into collectives. And every collective would be given a quota of food that it had to deliver to the state. A quota it could not produce. The military and secret police moved into the farming areas to ensure that all the food was taken. Anyone, who was accused of hoarding food, was executed.

During the harvest of 1932 and into 1933, the people just across the border had all their food taken from them. They were left with nothing to eat and were not allowed to leave. At least 7 million people in the Ukraine were starved to death that year, one quarter of the population of the Ukraine.

We had heard these stories but it had been hard to believe that anyone would commit such a crime. Until we saw the desolation ourselves from our trains. These years were known as the time "when no bird sang". The people were so hungry that even a small songbird that ventured into the area would be captured and eaten.

In other, nearby, rural areas another 6 million people had been starved to death.

When the Russians took over Poland, they immediately dismantled the factories to take back to Russia. They were moved, by train, to the border but had to be unloaded and wait for the wider gauge Russian trains to pick them up. Both sides of this town were already piled high with all sorts of metal and machinery as well as our field crops. All were left on the ground; unprotected from the elements.

For two days, we traveled like this, keeping alive by boiling and drinking the water that we brought with us, until the wood ran out. Then it became cold. It was very cold.

It was late afternoon on the second day when the train was stopped and the doors were opened for the first time. Soldiers came to check their "passengers". The first baby had died in our car and was ripped away from his mother and thrown into a snow bank. This was just the first of many deaths.

Every siding, where we stopped, was piled with wood to power the trains. There would be a hut or two made of logs with a straw roof at each stop. Occasionally, we would see a horse or a cow trying to get shelter against the house. I never saw a barn.

At this first stop, two men would be ordered out of each car and told to bring in wood and water for the next part of our journey.

During the next days we stopped often; usually to let other trains go by. The Russians had invaded Finland and the Finns were fighting hard. 68,000 Soviet troops would be killed. Many more would be injured.

Trains were taking the wounded, back south. Even though many times we were stopped for hours, the doors were not always opened. If we were allowed to go out for wood, the soldiers had to guard us and they preferred to stay inside their cars.

Whenever a soldier passed by, I would yell to him in Russian and Ukrainian asking that we be let out. When this proved fruitless, we managed to remove a window and hold a small boy outside. He undid the bolt, from the door, and let us out. One of the men took the bolt and threw it into the snow. But a guard saw us and quickly called his commander.

To my surprise, I realized that the commander was the same lieutenant that had been in our house. He recognized me and came to talk to me.

He warned me, "If any one tries to run away, the guards have been ordered to shoot them."

But I showed him the desolation around the tracks. "Where could we possibly run to?! In this cold, we would freeze to death before we found any type of shelter."

He finally agreed not to bolt the doors and to allow us out at every stop for food and water. Then I asked about food. I was told that we would be fed the next time we reached a large town.

That night, as we slept, the doors were bolted shut again. At the next station, we couldn't get out. That was it. We beat at the sides of the car. One man had smuggled a small axe aboard and he began chopping a hole through the door.

The Commandant came running. He was surprisingly calm. He finally agreed to try and keep us in as good a condition as he could for the rest of the trip. He left and arranged to get us some weak soup. This was our first meal. We would eventually get two more meals of soup, a half kilogram of bread and, as a treat, 100 grams of sugar. That was all the food we would get during the entire trip. We couldn't get at our food locked in the last cars.

We kept traveling north and east. There was no doubt now. We were heading for Siberia.

When we finally reached the forests of Siberia, it was like nothing any of us had ever seen before. It was like the forests of the nursery rhymes we were read. The forests that held witches and ogres. The forests that, once you entered, you never left. From a hill, we saw a land of trees extending in every direction as far as the eye could see.

The only break, in this picture, was a single train track disappearing deep into the forest. The track that we were on.

We were still west of the Ural Mountains. Geographically, Siberia is all the land east of the Urals whether the land is forest, desert or Arctic. But to the people, who were deported to these isolated areas, the desert was the desert, the Arctic was the Arctic and the land that was completely forested was Siberia. This was a part of what would be called the Gulag Archipelago.

After 15 days, the train stopped and everyone was ordered off. We were in a clearing of about 25 houses. The name on the station was Pinyug. It must have been a major stop. Wood, for the trains, was piled several rows deep on both sides of the tracks.

It was mid afternoon but we were so far north that it was already dark. Again, horse drawn sleighs were waiting for us. The Commandant told us that the men were to wait here while these sleighs took the women and children to our new homes.

It took only an hour for the sleighs to return. We unloaded all our belongings from the train to the sleighs.

"This is the last trip that we're making." We were told. "So you'll have to walk the rest of the way."

About four kilometers later, we came to another clearing in the bush where the women and children were waiting for us. In the center, of the clearing, stood three long log barracks. Russian militia soldiers rounded us up and led us to these barracks. Our family was taken to the biggest one.

It was an old building lit by naphtha lamps. There were boards all along the wall that would serve as our beds. In the center was a stove and a pile of wood.

"Get your pots and come outside for some kipiatok." We were told.

We didn't know the word but it had to be some sort of Russian food. We came to a large barrel where we were given some hot water and signaled to move on. Everyone waited for something more. When nothing else came, someone asked a soldier what we were supposed to do with the water.

"Drink it," he said, "because today you will get nothing more."

My mother started complaining. Then everyone was yelling. "For fifteen days, you have kept us in that train with almost nothing to eat. It would be better if you would kill us now rather than to slowly starve us to death."

We were promised bread the next day. We didn't know, yet, that bread was the most treasured item in Russia. It could keep you alive or you could trade it for almost anything else that you needed.

We had little choice. We went back to our barracks and tried to sleep. As soon as we lay down, we felt a pricking sensation. Just a little at first but we soon felt it on our entire bodies. We grabbed the lamps to see what was happening. The sleeping boards were covered with bed bugs. Parasites.

This was our welcome to Siberia.

Chapter Two – The First Year-Spring 1940

They left us alone for the next two days. On the third day, a group of soldiers came into our barracks and started picking out the stronger men. From the approximately 1,000 people in the camp, they finally rounded up 80 to 90 men including me and my brother Eddie, who was only 17 years old at the time. We were told that we were going into the forest.

It was extremely cold with the snow coming up to our waists. Since we had never experienced this kind of weather in Poland, we didn't have the boots or the clothing for this climate.

As we made our way through the snow, each man would take a turn in front to make a path for the others to follow. It was hard work and it took us almost two hours to travel half a kilometer. The Russian soldiers, who were leading us, had short but wide skis. They worked like snowshoes and the soldiers were able to move easily on top of the snow.

Meanwhile, those persons who were left at the camp were also put to work. Some had to cut trees, which were near the camp, to be used for firewood. Others were put to work fixing the barracks. These barracks were in poor shape. The walls had been simply made from the logs that had been cut to make this clearing. The logs were still green when they were used and shrank as they dried. This left large holes between the logs. The holes had been patched with moss that was gathered nearby. But the birds, mice and insects kept pulling this moss out so that it was impossible to keep the walls patched.

In the forest, the soldiers explained what was expected from us. We would have to cut at least the Soviet "norm" each day or they wouldn't supply us with bread (food). This norm was seven and a half-cubic meters of wood per person; cut down, cleared of branches, cut to measure, piled and the branches burned. This was to be a minimum because they said that a Russian could make two or three norms per day. We would be paid seven and half rubles for the first norm we made each day. We would get fifty per-cent more for a second norm and double for any extra that we would cut. But that first day we cut only a few trees. We made a fire and packed the snow to mark where we would work the next day. The next day we would start for good.

The next day we were given wooden shovels. We couldn't use metal shovels because the snow would freeze to the metal. We had to clear the snow from around each tree before we could cut it. Each tree had to be cut no more than sixteen inches from the ground. The logs would be pulled out later by horses and, if the stumps were any higher, it would be hard to maneuver the horses.

They formed us into seven man brigades. One man would fell the trees with an elbow saw, two would clean off the branches, two would cut the trees into proper lengths and stack it, and the last man would burn the branches and remove the snow from the next tree to be cut. We would work ten hours a day, mostly in the dark, so we needed the fires to see. Russian soldiers traveled between the groups to make sure that everyone was working.

This was virgin forest. Because of the climate, the trees grew very slowly and the wood was very hard. The spruce trees, that we were to cut, were thirty to forty inches in diameter and twenty feet high. Each tree had thousands of branches growing the entire length of the trunk. And every branch had to be cut off. Birch, poplar and pine also grew in the area. They grew twice as high and didn't have the number of branches that the spruce had but we weren't working on them.

Each man, who would be working in the bush, was given a half-kilo of bread each morning. We would take some of this bread to work with us. This bread was never fully baked and it acted like a sponge. If you squeezed it, water would run out. So, in the winter, it would freeze into a block of ice.

There would be a Russian keeping a large pot of water heating in the center of the work camp. He would keep melting snow to provide us with drinking water. When we wanted to eat our bread, we might push it onto a stick and hold it in the fire until it had thawed. More often we would simply put a piece into a cup of hot water and then eat the portion that would melt.

For the first few weeks, no one made his quota of wood so we were given no money, and if we wanted to buy bread it cost us one-rubble ten kopiejek per kilo. The bread was half rye, half barley and half-raw. It was so heavy that one-kilo was a small loaf; smaller than a loaf of store bread today. Each working man was given half a loaf but the rest of the people were given only 200 grams each. In other words, one loaf for five people. We were also given a bowl of barley soup six nights a week. We didn't work on Sunday so we were given bread but no soup. Occasionally, they added fish to the soup. Sometimes, it would be minnows, whole and un-cleaned. Other times it was a fish that no one had seen before. Actually, it was only fish heads. But these heads looked like a horse's head and were about the same size. For the first three weeks, no one could buy any extra food.

We would end up sweating profusely by the end of the workday. There was no time or place to dry ourselves off. By the time we returned to the barracks, we were so exhausted that, after having a little soup, we fell asleep. We brought spruce branches and moss back with us and put these on our sleeping boards to make them a little softer. But it was still always cold in the barracks. We had people keeping the stove burning all night long but everyone had to sleep with their clothes on. I didn't have a winter hat and could only wear my army beret to sleep. By morning, my hair would be frozen solid. I worked like this for only one week.

After only one week I became very sick. It felt as if my head was frozen solid. I cleaned myself up as best I could, put on my uniform and went to see the camp doctor. The doctor was a woman and she simply said that I didn't look sick to her. I did have a high temperature so she gave me an aspirin and told me to sleep it off. For the next two weeks I couldn't do a thing. I probably had pneumonia. These two weeks I spent day and night sitting in front of the stove, sleeping only half an hour at a time. I found a few rocks and heated them up by placing them on top of the stove. Then, I would wrap them in wet towels and place them against my head. It was as if someone was hammering against my skull. The pain was excruciating. For the next seventy years, when my head would become too cold this pain would return.

We stayed in this camp for only three weeks. During this time, we arranged ourselves into "family" units. Those people who didn't have any families in the camp set up their beds next to their friends. Plus we made friends with the people who lived around us. During the time I was sick, I was able to get to know many of the teenagers. Only a few persons under 18 were given work in the bush. Among these teens there were five girls who had no one and became a family unit. Their leader was Antonina Woszczyaska, an attractive blonde, who would be noticed shortly.

The camp Commandant would walk through our barracks every day. He was always taking notes. Three weeks after our arrival we were told not to go into the bush. Twenty sleighs arrived early in the morning. The Commandant came to me and said that he needed an interpreter. He then brought out the book with the notes that he had been taking. I saw that he had marked who had become close in the past three weeks. These friends were to be split up again. Even the five teenaged girls would not be allowed to stay together. We were told to pack all of our belongings because the people that he had chosen would be moved again.

Again the people became agitated and told me to tell him that they wouldn't be split up like this.

I went to him and asked, "Why are you splitting up our families like this?"

He replied very sharply, "You are now in Russia and this is how things are done here!"

I explained to him, "We are not Russian. We are Polish. We are not prisoners but rather we are your 'special guests'. We don't want to be treated in the Russian way. If you continue to treat us like this, you will have trouble. If you take into account how we feel, it will be easier on us and therefore it will be easier on you."

He finally allowed some of these friendship groups to remain united.

The five girls were allowed to remain a family. I wanted my uncle and his family to remain with our family. But the Commandant wouldn't allow this. He said that, since my uncle spoke Russian, he would stay behind. I would go with him to our next camp.

We put the women, small children and our belongings into the sleighs. The rest of us walked behind. This included soldiers, cooks and office personnel who would help run the new camp. I walked at the back of the column and eventually began talking with an older Russian man. He was to be our doctor. As we talked, I learned that his name was Dr. Przeniezny and that he was from a Polish family that had been deported to the Soviet Union decades ago. He then told me that the Commandant was also from a Polish family. His name was Ivan Zborowski. From this day on, I felt more confident when dealing with the Commandant.

We traveled for at least ten kilometers until we reached another clearing. It was about ten hectares in size and had a stream running through it. This stream would become a raging river in the spring as the snow melted and became only a trickle by late summer. There were three barracks on one side of the stream and two more on the other, connected by a bridge. They would eventually bring about 600 people here.

There were over 100 families taken from our village. In our first camp, there were 35 of these families with us. Now, there were only 7 families here from our village. Along with us there were the Grzejoczyk family (5 members), the Stolbon family (5 members), the Jarosz family (7 members), the Chudzik family (8 members), the Szafans who were newlyweds and the Uchmans who were also recently married and would soon have their first child in this camp.

Once again, Lt. Zborowski pulled out his notes and began assigning us to the barracks according to his list. The people asked me to talk to him again. They didn't like the way he was organizing them.

Finally, Zborowski told me, "place them wherever you want. Just give me a list of where everyone is."

We were told that this was the place we would all die. One of the more arrogant Russian soldiers told us that we would never be allowed to leave this region unless we volunteered for the Soviet army.

I asked him, "What if we join the Polish army?"

He simply answered, "There is no Polish army. Poland is dead. The Soviet Union will never allow Poland to live again."

The Soviets were trying to make a second, more secure rail line to the northern port of Arkhangel'sk. Arkhangel'sk was a secure exit for the Soviets into the Barents Sea and therefore into the north Atlantic. Because the Gulf Stream brought warm water north of the Scandinavian countries the port could be kept open most of the year.

The Soviets had started making railways into the north in 1920 using forced labor and they were still expanding them in 1940. They had direct lines from Moscow to Arkhangel'sk and to Murmansk. Now they were building a rail line from Kirov, which is over 800 kilometers east of Moscow, to the northern ports.

The land was hilly and they used forced labor to knock down the hills and fill in the valleys using only picks and shovels to move the earth. They had no nails and had to drill holes into the logs of their bridges and use wooden pegs to hold them together.

There was a large swamp, in our region, feeding streams that were a source of the Divina River. This swamp was fed by hot springs so it remained unfrozen all year round. Already, there had been 3 roads built through this swamp. They linked small, nameless villages but were only strong enough to handle foot traffic and small wagons. Moscow wanted a rail line to cross the swamp. Central Planning dictated that the rail line would go through the swamp.

Immediately after the Russian revolution, the Communists rounded up all Roman Catholic priests as well as those Orthodox priests who didn't support the revolution. Large numbers were sent to the Pinyug camps. They were given the job of building this rail line. The first train to use their newly built line managed to travel 200 meters into the swamp. The tracks gave way and the train fell onto its side. The priests were blamed for this failure and they ended up in mass graves only 300 meters from our barracks.

It would now be our job to provide the wood to build the rail line. But now, the rail line would go around the swamp.

On the second day, after arriving, we were called out into the yard. They again formed us into brigades. This time, they put 5 men and 2 women into each brigade because in Russia everyone was equal and women were expected to work. They took each foreman into the woods and gave each brigade a separate area to cut. We would no longer all cut in the same area but rather be assigned different areas around the camp.

Into my brigade, they assigned my brother Eddie, my father, John Grzegorczy from our village, John Ptak an older man and a strong woman Aniela Bema. They also gave us two 16-year-old girls, the younger John's sister Wladka and my sister Sofie. We had an extra girl because they were under 18 and they found it difficult clearing the snow from around the trees. Because we now had 8 people in our brigade, we would have to prepare 60 cubic meters of wood per day. That was impossible in the winter and, even in the summer, only occasionally would a brigade meet its quota. So it started out badly and progressively got worse.

On April 9, Germany invaded Denmark and Norway. The Danish army put up a spirited defense for almost a minute. Within 4 hours Denmark had surrendered. Norway surrendered soon afterward but individual Norwegian forces continued retreating north for 2 months before surrendering. The British navy was too slow to react.

In the barracks, most of the people were ethnic Poles but there were a few Ukrainian families mixed in. Everyone got along well with the exception of 2 Ukrainian families who were allowed to form their own work brigade. They were 5 strong men and 2 daughters who would have nothing to do with the rest of us. They spent their time with each other and with the Russian soldiers. They were the only families who were allowed to receive parcels from the outside. They were given the best areas to cut, near a local village, and often made their quota of wood.

Towards the middle of April, we noticed that those 2 families had fresh food. The Russians were allowing them to go to the village and trade with the villagers.

Antonina Woszczynska was brave or somewhat reckless. Her father had been a bureaucrat and had been one of the first Poles to be arrested after the Russian invasion — never to be seen again. When the Russians came to move her, she refused to budge until they allowed her to take all her family possessions. She remained firm and eventually was supplied with 3 sleighs. She was now the richest person in the camp (with the exception of the 2 anti social Ukrainian families). Antonina was the first one of us to follow the Ukrainians and find the village. She was able to trade for some food. For this, the Russians threw her into the local jail. The rest of the camp protested and she was released the next day. She would be the only one of us to spend a day in jail.

Immediately, everyone learned where the village was located. But we were still forbidden from going to the village under the threat of death. The food that we had brought from Poland was gone and the Russians didn't feed us properly. We were starving. People who weighed 100 kilos, only a few months ago, now weighed as little as 50 kilos. So we had no choice. Soon every family was sending someone to the village to trade for food. Eventually, the Russians relented and, because they couldn't stop us, allowed us to trade openly.

This local village, with no name, was a collective farm established by prisoners during the time of the Tsars. They could keep a small garden, 1 cow, 1 goat and a few chickens for their own use. In return they paid an annual tax of 20 kilos of butter, 30 kilos of meat and, for each chicken, 30 eggs. The villagers were poor and wanted everything that we offered in trade. They wanted our clothes (especially underwear), any rings or watches, shoes, spoons, knives, etc. For a pail, one man received 2 pails of potatoes. We traded mostly for grain and potatoes but occasionally did get some luxuries as meat, butter and eggs. This is the food that allowed us to survive.

The Russians didn't treat their animals any better than they treated us. They always had horses, at the camps, to pull the wood out of the bush. They never used wagons. Instead, they would place a log on the ground and tie poles to the log. They would load this with the wood we cut and the horses would drag the load to the railway.

The Russians handlers would collect branches from birch trees and tie them into bundles to dry in the sun. The horses would graze on local grass during the summer but during the long winter they had nothing to eat but these branches.

I remember one horse in particular. One day they brought in a magnificent white stallion. He was the most beautiful animal I have ever seen in my life. He was a spirited animal and didn't want to pull the log skids. He fought his handlers at first. But after a few days without food and water he began giving in. Within two months, he was nothing but skin and bones. He hung his head low and did whatever his handlers demanded. There was no life left in him.

When spring came, so did the black flies. Every clearing was black with them. We needed to keep the fires smoking to keep them away while we worked. When the snow disappeared, we were able to explore around our new camp. This is when we found the train that had fallen into the swamp. We also found the graves of the Russian priests who worked here before us.

More importantly, we found a rich valley. In this valley, stood a dark green carpet of grass. We asked the Russians for a couple of scythes because we wanted to harvest this grass. They didn't want to give them to us until we convinced them that 2 Poles with scythes couldn't overpower 25 Russian soldiers with rifles. We cut the grass and put it in windrows to dry. The days were now long and it never rained during the summer so we made excellent hay. The ground remained wet because the water couldn't drain off through the permafrost. We managed to get a harvest every few weeks; the grass grew so fast.

The work was very hard. In the swamp, there were mounds of dry ground. We had to balance ourselves on these mounds to cut the grass. On occasion, when we fell off, we ended up knee deep in mud and water. And the black flies! They covered our bodies. We had to put veils over our heads to keep the flies out of our eyes and mouths. It was the only way we could see or breathe. This would be the first time that the horses would have hay during the winter. We had all worked with horses and felt that these noble beasts needed to be treated humanely.

It seems that the Russian villagers had never considered using this grass to feed their animals. They used the Russian system of feeding them branches from the forest though they did add wheat straw to their diets. The growing season was extremely short but the villagers could grow wheat. They would plant wheat in the spring. The grain would germinate slowly and reach a height of a few inches by the time winter arrived. It would then lie dormant under the snow over the winter. The wheat would grow rapidly the next year, with up to 20 hours of sunlight, and was ready for harvest by September. The next summer, the villagers began harvesting hay for themselves.

Our first harvest brought something unexpected. Once we removed the first cut of grass, we saw that the ground was dark red. It was in fact covered with red berries. We had discovered a cranberry bog. The cranberries from last season were still there for the picking. And we picked them. They were too sour to eat raw in any quantity so we put them into our soup. They were still sour but at least they were better than nothing and we needed the vitamin C in them.

The bog seemed endless and we picked barrels of berries. We soon found out, much to our delight, that the Russian office staff wanted to buy our cranberry harvest and ship it to Moscow. For 2 hours of picking, a man could make 5 rubbles. This compared to 7 1/2 rubbles he might (but seldom did) make, if he was lucky, for 10 hours of backbreaking work in the forest.

In the fall, we discovered that the forest was full of blueberries. The cranberries were at least 2 kilometers from our camp but the blueberries were almost outside our doors. There were blueberries in almost every clearing but the richest harvest came from around the mass graves of the priests. Again we picked. They tasted much better than the cranberries. What we didn't eat, we sold to the Russians.

We had to work 6 days a week. On Saturday evenings and Sundays we worked for ourselves. That is when we went to the local village or harvested our "crops". We were then asked to put up another building. The Russians would send educators on occasion to teach us about the joys of Communism and they needed a place to hold the meetings. The rest of the time, we could use it as a meeting hall for ourselves. So we agreed.

On May 10th, Germany invaded Belgium and the Netherlands. Finally, the British launched air raids against German roads, rail lines and cities. By May 14th all Dutch resistance had ceased. Britain and France sent troops to Belgium to little avail. The Germans marched on. On May 26, the British, surrounded, began evacuating their troops from Dunkirk. On June 14, the Germans entered Paris and France was ready to surrender. French troops celebrated the end of their war with toasts of champagne.

Thousands of Polish soldiers had fled to France to continue fighting Hitler. They were astonished that the French would surrender so easily, without a fight. They were further disillusioned when the French soldiers ordered the Poles to surrender and be taken as prisoners to the Germans. Fortunately, the French were no better at fighting the Poles than they were fighting the Germans. The Polish soldiers refused to surrender and fled to Britain; leaving the French soldiers cowering in their camps, awaiting their new Nazi masters.

On June 17, Moscow announced that Latvia, Lithuania and Estonia would come under Soviet domination and invaded.

Europe was now controlled by the German-Russian alliance.

It was early one Sunday morning in mid June when the men were called out of the barracks. They selected 34 of the stronger young men and took us back to Pinyug. Here we were put on a train and shipped north to the town of Luza. This was again just a place for the trains to stop and pick up wood. They put us in barracks that the Russians kept for forced labor crews.

The next morning they gave us axes and saws and took us several kilometers on foot into the forest. The road we walked on was rather unusual. It was made entirely of wood. It consisted of 2 tracks; each one made of 3 logs laid lengthwise. The Russians wanted to take logs from this area and they were using trucks. They didn't have gasoline here so the trucks were adapted to run on wood. A burner was installed to burn 3 or 4-inch blocks of birch wood. This would produce fumes that were pushed into the engine. The engine then used this as fuel. The road acted like train tracks for the trucks. We were to extend this road.

They formed us into brigades and, leaving a policeman to watch us, told us to work. We had to cut, clean and dress the wood. We had to flatten 3 sides. From the fourth side we had to cut wedges that would be used to hold the logs in place thus forming the road. They wouldn't allow us to burn the branches because the forest here was too dry. Therefore, the black flies were so thick that we could hardly breathe. We got very little work done that day.

That evening, I went to the camp commander and told him that we couldn't go on like this. We had to get rid of the black flies. There were a number of metal barrels at the station. If we could start fires in these barrels and create smoke, we could get rid of them. None of the Russians had considered this. The black flies were there and the workers simply had to put up with them.

We were supposed to pull the logs to the road using manpower. This was all but impossible to do. But they had horses at the camp. I asked the commander to give us a couple of these horses because one man with one horse could do the job much better. I also said that we'd like to get rid of this damn brigade system and organize ourselves into groups to do the work our way. Among us, there were several men who knew how to do this type of work. We were supposed to work 7 days a week but we wanted our Sundays off. Finally, I said that we didn't need the policemen watching over us. He actually agreed to give us everything we asked for, as long as we did a good job.

Now that we were free of Russian supervision, we worked in one group. When we needed the trees cut, a couple men would grab a saw and fell a few trees. Once we had our horses, it took only one man to drag the log to the road. Here several men would cut the logs into their proper shape. Finally, a crew of 4 men would use levers to place these finished logs into their proper position. Before long, we were very good at our respective jobs. The road that we laid was much better than the one laid previously.

The landscape was hilly and the road had to follow these contours. At the end of the road, they would place a large platform on which the trucks could turn around. The system worked well unless 2 trucks met going in opposite directions. Because of the hills, the driver of the one truck found it hard to see the other truck until they were only a few hundred meters apart. The empty truck would have to back up to where it started, no matter how far that was. So we decided to put in a siding, similar to the ones used by trains, to allow one truck to pull over and allow the other to pass.

I was part of the crew that dressed the logs. In Poland, my father had made an axe from "diamond" steel. It was the same metal that was used to make drill bits that were used for deep drilling. It was sharp enough to cut through stone. I brought it here with me and it was the only good axe we had. It was so valuable to me that I never let anyone else use it and always slept with it. I kept this axe with me throughout the entire war, later even taking it to the front with me and eventually bringing it to Canada. I finally lost it in Welland when someone "borrowed" it from a building site.

The Russians supplied us with 2-headed axes. They were said to be the best axes in the Soviet Union because they had been imported from Canada. They were so heavy and clumsy that no one could use them to dress logs properly. I showed the commander my axe. He was genuinely impressed and promised to find us some one-headed axes. They weren't as good as mine, but they allowed us to do a good job.

On the second Saturday after arriving at Luza, I asked the camp commander to allow me to go to Pinyug to see my family. I promised to be back by Monday morning. He told me that he couldn't give me a pass but I was free to try it if I wanted. Every train stopped here as well as in Pinyug. He simply warned me not to get on any train that was carrying Russian soldiers.

That evening, after work, I went to the station and climbed aboard the first southbound train. The conductor saw me and asked where I was going. I showed him my axe and told him that I was being sent to Pinyug to cut wood. This seemed to satisfy him and I was allowed to stay on board.

I was on the bridge between the barracks when the Commandant first noticed me. He was shocked to see me and rushed over to see what was going on. I told him that the commander of the other camp had given me a pass and sent his appreciation for the good workers that Zborowski had sent him. He simply smiled and went on his way. I would make this same trip every Sunday.

Towards the end of June, we witnessed a train heading north. It had between 50 to 60 cars of Polish civilians. We were not allowed to get close to the cars. But we knew what was in store for them.

We worked at Luza for 5 weeks. The length of the road was doubled during this time. In mid July we were sent back to Pinyug.

During that time, the men left behind had begun to salvage the tracks as well as the rail cars that were still in the swamp. Eventually, we would build a rail line from our camp to Pinyug. Before, one horse could only drag a few logs to the train station. But now we could use a team of horses to pull a rail car loaded with several hundred logs.

Zborowski told us we were going to build a bakery. The bread that we were being sent was so bad that even the Russians didn't want to eat it. There were bakers among the prisoners and they would prepare the bread. The Russian cooks had already been replaced by cooks that the prisoners supplied.

As a reward, we would also be allowed to set up a school for the children.

During the summer, the German air force attacked Britain in force. Thousands of civilians died from the bombing but the RAF downed over 1,300 German aircraft during the Battle of Britain. Large numbers of R.A.F. pilots came from other countries, including from Poland.

Polish pilots made up 20% of the RAF fighter squads. The British were losing the air war until the Polish airmen were allowed to fight. Soon these Polish pilots were the toast of England. Polish airmen were "adopted" by British celebrities and aristocrats, including Virginia Cherrill. Virginia, an American born actress, became world famous when she played the part of the blind girl in Charlie Chaplin's celebrated movie "City Lights." Virginia had a penchant for marrying well. Her second husband was famous movie star Cary Grant, to whom she was married for only one year. Her current husband was the Earl of Jersey, one of the richest men in England. When she married the Earl, she officially became known as the Countess of Jersey. Virginia's marriage to the Earl ended shortly after the war and her fourth and final husband, Florian Martini, was one of the Polish fighter pilots from her "adopted" squadron. Virginia and Florek were married for 48 years, until her death in 1996.

Hitler would abandon his attempt to conquer Britain and turn his attention to southeastern Europe.

Above – Left to Right: Our Family – Dan, Adela, Rick, Joe and Gary
Below – Left to Right: Loni, Joe and Sophie

Above – Sophie and Mother
Below – Left: Eddie Right: Loni

Above Left: Dolek, Above Right: Bolek, Below - Left to Right: Dolek, Eddie and Bolek

Above – Left to Right: The Countess of Jersey, The Earl of Jersey, Lady Caroline Child-Villiers, the Earl of Jersey's daughter, John Child-Villiers, (son of Squadron Leader The Hon. E.M. Child-Villiers, the Earl's brother), apprentice Dolek Dobrucki and apprentice Janek Mazur.

Above Right – The Countess of Jersey and children walking in the grounds of Richmond Palace, Richmond, Surrey.

Below Right – A drawing session. The Countess of Jersey, Lady Caroline Child-Villiers, apprentice Janek Mazur, Elizabeth McQueen (daughter of the butler to the Jersey's, now Sgt. McQueen in the Middle East, apprentice Dolek Dobrucki and John Child-Villiers (son of Squadron Leader The Hon. E.M. Child Villiers, the Earl's brother).

Walerian Joseph Dobrucki

Walerian Joseph Dobrucki with the Army in Egypt

Walerian Joseph Dobrucki with the Army in Ancona, Italy

Chapter Three – Winter 1940-41

In our region of Siberia, it almost never snowed. The ocean currents brought warm water around Norway and Finland into the Barents Sea. The waters remained ice-free most of the year. The winds would pick up this warm, moist air and push it inland. By the time this air reached us, it produced a constant ice fog. The ice crystals would float above us and eventually would drop to the ground. By the end of winter, there would be a flat 4 to 5 feet of snow covering the ground.

It was our Sunday off, late in November, when I was called into the Commandant's office.

"Do you know who Stachonov was?" He asked.

Of course I knew. Every Russian and everyone who lived near Russia knew the tales of Stachonov. He was a fictional character, from Russia's revolution, who could out-produce any other worker. He could cut more trees, harvest more grain, mine more ore than any other human being. Every Communist, in Russia, was pushed to be like Stachonov: to outdo each other.

"You Poles haven't been keeping up with your quotas."

How could we? Every time any group neared its quota, the men would be split up and replaced with girls or young boys. Even if they were well fed, no youngster could keep up with the amount of wood that had to be cut. And none of us were well fed.

"Well, I'm going to change that. I'm sending you to the Stachonov course. There, you'll learn the proper method of working with trees. You will learn how to meet your quota."

"Take 2 men and be ready to leave next Sunday." He told me.

I picked Janac Grzegorezyk and Szafran Wladk and we were ready when a sleigh pulled up the following week. The driver, a man called Sacharov, was one of our regular guards. He had a rifle sitting next to him so we hesitated getting in.

"Don't worry." He said while looking at the rifle. "The gun is for the wolves: not for you."

Since the Russians took over Poland, they were systematically eliminating our leaders. Thousands of military officers had already been murdered. Thousands more would be murdered. But, I suppose, we weren't important enough. And the wolves really were dangerous.

The story goes that ever since the dark ages, when the black plague hit Europe, wolves had learned to enjoy human flesh. You didn't wander far from inhabited areas without a weapon of some sort. Especially in winter, in the Arctic where there are only a few hours of daylight.

A dirt road ran along the train tracks in the center of a 100-meter wide path cut through the forest. We followed this road for 12 km. without seeing another person. Then we veered into the forest and traveled another 3km. before we reached a clearing.

Sacharov stopped to let us view this model camp. "Now you're going to see how real Soviet people work." He beamed proudly.

I couldn't see anything to be very proud of. There were 3 log barracks, newer, but otherwise no different than those we were kept in. We could see a few gangs of men moving in and out. But there was one innovation. Instead of the horses we used to pull out our logs, they had tractors. They had tractors that, like tanks, were on metal tracks. These men had no trouble moving their logs.

We were led into the first of the barracks. It was little different than our own.

"Grab an empty space." We were told as we were shown the sleeping boards along the walls. "And get yourselves a cup of water."

The cauldron, in the center of the room, held hot water and we needed it after out long cold trip. It was ready for the men who were now coming in from the forest. They even worked on Sundays.

"This is your Brigadier." We were shown a tall stout man among the workers. "He is our best worker. He will teach you how to work."

The Brigadier saw us. He appeared cheerful and was smiling as he approached us. He shook our hands, embraced us and gave us a warm reception in a very un-Soviet like style.

"Come. I'll take you for supper." He said.

He took us to the cafeteria where we dined on millet soup and a slice of bread. After supper, he took us to a storage room to get us a saw and axe. Then we were given heavy, but warm, coats and boots for which we had to pay. Fortunately, we had some money from the cranberries we had sold that past summer.

"You'll need these if you want to keep up with the other men. Be ready to work at 6 o'clock." He told us.

I assume it was 6 o'clock when we were awoken. The only light outside was from the stars, the northern lights and a few bonfires in the yard. Dawn was still several hours away.

The Brigadier gave us each a small can and told us to fill it with the still warm water.

"Make sure you keep it filled all day." He told us. "Maybe, you want some Russian coffee with that." He offered.

I hadn't had any coffee of any sort since we were taken from Poland. "I've never heard of Russian coffee but I'm sure it'll be better than plain water."

He pulled out a small package. It contained cooked barley mixed with some dried fruits. He put a portion into each can. This was our coffee.

Everyone from the barracks went to the same clearing. Three of the girls began making a fire as we sat down for breakfast. We were each given half a loaf of bread. This and our 'coffee' would have to last us till the end of the day and our supper of millet soup.

"Keep your coffee cans next to the fire." We were told. "Drink as much as you can and keep it filled with snow. You'll need your coffee to survive."

We were ready for our first lesson in the Stachonov system. The trees, which they wanted us to cut, had already been marked. To my surprise, all the snow and undergrowth next to the trees, that we were about to cut, had been cleared. We were going to be cutting pine. The trees were tall and free of branches up to their very crowns.

"You have to know what a tree wants to do." Offered the Brigadier. "Every tree wants to fall in a certain direction. It's up to you to ignore what the tree wants and to make it fall where you want it to fall."

He picked a tree and showed us that, if it fell in the direction it was leaning, it would get caught in the other trees. But, if it fell the way that you wanted, it would fall all the way to the ground without getting caught on another tree. Then, using an axe, he cut a large "V" into the side of the tree trunk that faced the direction he wanted it to fall.

Another man took a saw and began cutting into the tree on the side opposite the "V" cut. When the saw was far enough into the tree, a third man put a wedge into the saw cut and hammered the wedge into the tree. The wedge opened a larger space for the saw and forced the tree to lean into the "V" cut. Two more men, each with a 10-foot pike, pushed the tree in the direction it was supposed to fall. In minutes, the pine was on the ground: in the exact spot that it was meant to be.

The other marked trees had "V"s cut into the side facing the fallen pine. One by one they were felled, falling across the trunk of the first pine. Now the branches could be removed while they were still off the ground.

We began to work and, as we came to our lunch break, we had dozens of 35-foot long trees cut.

"When do we cut them to size?" I asked.

"These trees will be used for ships or for electric poles or for those bridges they're building. We don't cut them any shorter." Said the Brigadier.

"Who pays for the people who cleared the snow for us? And who clears the underbrush? Who marks the trees that we're to cut? Who pays for the girls to watch the fire? Who takes the trees away once they're cut?" I needed to know.

"One thing has nothing to do with the other." He answered. "Another crew is paid to prepare the site for us. All you need to do is to cut the trees. That's your only job."

I explained, to him, how we were forced to work at our camp. Each crew, including youngsters, did everything from preparing the site to cutting the trees and moving them to the train station. And all the logs had to be cut into short logs.

He stared in disbelief. "It's no wonder you can't produce your norm. When you get back, show your Commandant the right way to work."

Three of the trees, that we had just cut, more than made up a norm. Finally, I understood how some people could survive by cutting trees.

Later that evening, the Brigadier invited me for a talk. He and his wife had their own room at the end of the barracks. Inside they had a real stove, a small table with a bench, some pots and a working clock. At least he knew when it was 6 o'clock.

He brought out a bottle of vodka. His wife brought us a pot of kluski (a type of Polish noodle for soup) made with, hard to get, pork fat. We all ate from the same pot as we talked.

"My wife and I are both Poles." He began. "The Tsar sent us here years ago. These camps have been around forever. The Communists just continued using them. We've been told that you are bourgeoisie, large landlords. Is this true?"

When I told them what we had in Poland, what happened to us and what we lost, they cried.

His wife said, "My parents told me they heard that the Russians were expelling entire towns but I just couldn't believe it. How could the

Russians lie like that? They tell us that we have the best living conditions in the world. How can they keep doing this to us?"

"That's just the way the Russians are. They think of themselves as being the master race so they are allowed to do whatever they please; whatever they can get away with."

After working for 2 weeks, I decided to go back and see my family. I asked the Brigadier if I could have the next Sunday free.

The Brigadier didn't think it was such a good idea. "You won't catch any trains from here. It's a long walk especially in the cold. You'll be by yourself the entire way with all those wolves out there. And you have to be here for work."

But I was determined to go. I told him I would leave immediately after work on Saturday and be back by Monday morning. But I would take my axe with me, just in case.

The Brigadier brought me 2 kg. of millet, 1 kg. of fat and 2 kg. of kluski to take with me. I traveled on the tracks, which were kept clear of snow, and made it to our home camp about 2 a.m. on Sunday. I had to leave, again, that afternoon in order to reach the new work camp by Monday morning.

I finally realized what was happening to us. In my early 20's this trip shouldn't have been that hard on me. But, by the time I came back, I was exhausted. I was so weak that I knew I couldn't survive another trip like this. The supplies we brought from Poland and the berries we found in the woods were the only things that kept us alive this long.

After 3 weeks of work, Sacharov came with a sleigh to take us back. The Brigadier gave us a final glass of vodka. I apologized that I had nothing to give him for all his help and hospitality. We had worked a full 3 weeks but we were not paid for the work. It was supposed to be a learning experience.

The Brigadier wished us good luck. "I'm just glad I could help you." He said as we left.

Back at camp, Sacharov took us to the Commandant. He immediately wanted to know what we had learned.

We said, "they do everything differently there." And we explained what we had seen during the past 3 weeks.

The Commandant listened carefully. He said, "This is all new to me. No one told me that we are to provide crews to clear away the snow for you." He promised to look into it.

The next morning we were to demonstrate our newly learned techniques. In the forest, I picked out a pine. We dropped it without a snag and then felled other pines across its trunk. Since these trees were now off the ground, we easily cut off all the branches and pulled the trunk away. When we were finished, all that was left was a neat pile of branches ready to be burned.

"We don't need to cut these pines for firewood." I said. "The Soviets will take them in 40-foot lengths."

All the crews went to the dry pine growths and began cutting. We still had to clear our own snow but we easily reached our norms.

We were congratulated by "the Soviet" for making our norms "as well as any Soviet people".

As the winter progressed, the snow became deeper and we were forced to cut the shorter stands of poplar, birch and spruce again. We had no more 40-foot trees without branches. The spruce had to be cut into short logs and every one of the branches had to be removed.

And we couldn't remove the logs from the forest. The bark had to be removed from the logs but the bark would not come off a spruce log during the winter. We would have to wait until spring. When the thaw came and the sap began to run, the bark could be removed. Until then, we had to pile the logs and wait.

The winter was colder than anything we had ever experienced in Poland. Any winter clothing we had was inadequate and was quickly wearing out. The Russians sold us large rolls of 1/4-inch cotton cloth. We used this to make gloves, hats and to insulate our other clothes. When it came to winter boots, we turned to the forest. The bark from birch trees was cut into wide strips and molded onto people's feet in place of boots. The cotton cloth was soaked in water, wrapped in more bark and allowed to freeze. These boots would keep our feet from freezing. The bark from linden trees was soaked until it came apart in strips. These strips were used as rope to tie the bark and cloth boots tight.

All winter long, we waited for the Commandant to make changes according to his Stachanov system. These changes never came. We continued to prepare our own sites. We continued to have children in our work groups and they were expected to produce just as much as able-bodied adults.

When we were first deported to Siberia, we all had extra food and clothing that we had brought from home. When we didn't have enough money to buy the food that the Russians offered, we could trade for food with the villagers or borrow money or food from other families. The food, from home, went first. Our extra clothing had been traded or simply worn out. We made very little money cutting trees and were lucky to be able to get money by selling the cranberries and blueberries that we picked.

The people, who had it worst, were the families with members who couldn't work. My father, my brother Eddie and I worked cutting trees. My sister Sophie worked in our brigade, burning branches. My sister Loni was little more than a baby and our twin brothers Bolek and Dolek were too young to work. They were sick so often that our mother had to take care of them and couldn't work outside.

Most of the families couldn't buy enough bread or 'camp soup' under normal circumstances. It was worse during the winter. Every so often, the Russians decided to play games with our food.

We were normally sent dark barley bread that cost us 1.2 rubbles per kilo. Occasionally, they would send us white bread made from processed flour. It looked nicer but it cost us 3 rubbles per kilo. Many men didn't make 3 rubbles per day. We had the choice of buying white bread or having nothing. Either way, we went hungry.

The spruce logs were piling up. Since they couldn't be moved, the Russians came up with a system for the wood that we cut.

Marisha, one of the girls from our barracks, began working in the Commandant's office. Each day she would bring a Russian civilian, a log counter, into the forest. It was their job to mark the end of each log with red paint and to record it. We would be paid for every log that they recorded.

"How does the Russian work?" I asked her.

"He's lazy. He doesn't pay attention to what he's doing."

That's all I needed to know. One day, after they left, I went to a pile of logs with fresh red paint applied to their ends. I took my saw and cut off every painted end on that pile. Then I burned this painted wood.

Next day, the log counter returned, marked and recorded the pile again. They weren't going to pay us a survival wage but at least they would pay us twice for many of these logs.

Chapter Four – Another Year-Early 1941

Campaigning for re-election in October of 1940, Franklin Roosevelt declared, "I have said this before, but I shall say it again and again and again: your boys are not going to be sent into any foreign wars."

On January 6, after winning the election, Roosevelt asked Congress to approve giving arms credits to 'countries at war with aggressor nations'. On March 11, the lend-lease act was signed into law.

At the same time, Hitler was getting money for his war by selling millions of dollars worth of bonds to German Americans. These bonds would be repaid by the sale of captured lands and properties after the war. The Russians held our land but Hitler had plans for Russia.

We did put up the meeting hall that the Russians wanted. When it was finished, two Commissars came to give us lessons in the virtues of Communism. They arrived while we were in the forests so they went to check out our barracks. My mother was sick at the time and was resting inside.

The Commissars went to her and asked, "Do you know about the Soviet culture?"

"Oh, yes." She said showing them naphtha lamps without any glass covers. "We've been here for almost a year, waiting for you to deliver the glass for these lamps. But that is nothing. The bigger Russian culture is here."

She got up and pulled on a board in the wall and showed a wall full of bed bugs. Exposed to the light, the bed bugs fled into any cracks they could find. "Yes. I know all about Soviet culture.

The Commissars left and these two men never came back. Next day we got the glass for the lamps and sulpha with which we washed and fumigated the barracks. There was no further mention of Communist meetings in our new hall.

But the hall remained and we made good use of it. A few men had brought violins with them and lots of men had harmonicas. They would play their music and the teens would dance. No Russian ever came to these dances so we could hold our anti-Soviet meetings.

On Sundays, we used the building for washing. We would build a large fire and use it to heat stones. Then we would take these heated stones and drop them into wooden tubs of water. This would heat the water for bathing and it would create enough steam to allow the men to shave themselves.

Spring became very important to us. By April, the sun was out for more than half the day and the snow was melting. And the sap was running in the trees.

The bark was no longer frozen to the fallen spruce trees. It could finally be removed from the logs. With their axes, the men would cut through the bark the entire length of the log. Then everyone would grab the bark, along the cut edge, and pull. Even the children and old people joined in. The bark came off in strips of up to 3 or 4 meters. Where piles of logs had been, there was soon nothing but huge piles of bark.

Once the logs had been removed, the Commandant called me into his office where I was introduced to 2 new Soviet officers.

"The Commandant tells us that you have a large family to care for." One of them began. "Too many to feed on the wages you make. Well, we have a proposition for you.

You have a lot of bark from the spruce trees all around your camp. We need this bark for our tanneries. How would you like to have your mother and your little brothers and sister gather this bark for us?"

"How much would they be paid?" I asked.

"3 1/2 rubbles per cubic meter."

I was in shock. This was impossible. Gathering one cubic meter of bark would pay as well as cutting and preparing 3 cubic meters of wood. And it would be easy work. The bark was light and was already in large piles.

"How much bark do you want?" was all I needed to know.

"As much as you can provide."

"Can anyone gather it?"

"No. You have 3 young children in your family and a mother who can't do any other work. So only your family will be paid to supply the bark. They can easily gather all that we need."

"Can I at least help them?"

"You have your own work to do. But you can help after you finish your job and on Sundays."

All our people, from the camp, talked to me hoping that I would take their grievances to the Commandant. The Commandant was viewing me as their leader. He was worried that, if too many people would become agitated, he would have discipline problems. He had sent me away before. Now he would keep me occupied after hours and on Sundays.

I really had no choice but to go along with the deal.

We began gathering bark that evening and in one hour we had 2 cubic meters ready. This was worth a good day's wages working in the bush. We would bend the bark into one-meter cubes and use sticks to hold the cubes together. In the next few days we gathered 60 cubic meters of bark. And, while they were gathering the bark, my mother, Bolek, Dolek and Loni were each given a half kg. of bread daily, a worker's wage.

As we went to a new area, to cut pine, I noticed that other Soviet teams had cut and cored spruce trees that year. I asked the Commandant if we could gather this too.

He agreed.

In the next 3 weeks, we gathered over 160 cubic meters of bark. We were to be paid about 500 rubbles.

"Enough!" Yelled the Commandant. "No one in the Soviet Union can be allowed to make this much money."

We were eventually paid for the work we did. The Russians took some of the bark but left most of it behind.

Bolek and Dolek had been sick most of the time since we left home. They had the mumps and continued to have swollen glands, which made it hard for them to eat. At first, on the train and in Siberia, mother used some of the fat that we brought along. She would melt it in hot water to feed the twins. This worked while the fat lasted. Bolek remained sick.

Once we found the village with no name, we also found their cows. The villagers would put bells around their cows' necks and let them run loose, throughout the forest, to feed. When they needed to be milked, they would go back home.

At night, it would be easy to find them simply by listening for the sounds of their bells. I kept a bottle with me and would gather fresh grass in the evening. Then I would go looking for a cow. Whenever I found one, I would give it the grass and get a little bit of milk for my brothers.

The Russians began bringing in a few items into the store. My father took the money, from the bark we had gathered, and bought 4 pairs of rubber boots. He kept one pair and traded the other 3 pair to the villagers for a fresh goat. Now we would have milk for the summer.

That spring most of the soldiers, who were guarding us, left. Only 3 older soldiers and the bureaucrats, who ran the camp, remained. Now we had a lot more freedom.

There were a lot of rumors going around. The camp doctor told us anything that he heard. Marisha, working in the Commandants office, kept her ears open for whatever information she could hear. It seemed as if the soldiers were needed because the Russians were at war again.

It was June 22, 1941 when Germany launched the largest military attack in history against Soviet occupied Poland. The attack was meant to be launched earlier, but their Italian allies were having trouble trying to defeat the Greeks that spring. Hitler had to divert his troops to Greece. Now he was well behind schedule.

Finnish troops also moved into territory the Soviets Union had recently conquered. Britain immediately promised aid to the Soviets. Soon convoys were sent to Arkhangel'sk and Murmansk with military equipment and supplies.

We noticed that there were more trains going through Pinyug. We didn't know that the Russians were moving all their manufacturing plants east, towards the Ural Mountains. They were suffering heavy casualties in their fight against Finland. All the wounded soldiers were moved south through Pinyug. When we brought our wood to the railway station, we couldn't help but see these trains. And we could see that they were loaded with wounded soldiers.

At first, the Russians tried to keep us away from the trains. But there was no way of telling when another train would arrive with more wounded men. Finally, we were no longer permitted to bring our wood into Pinyug. Russian civilians now came to our camp and only they were allowed to move the wood back to the station.

During the summer, we would walk 4 km. from our camp to cut trees. Rather than going back every night, I built myself a small hut at the work site. I would stay there several nights a week. The Russians continued to record and mark the logs that we cut. I continued to cut off these marked ends. And it gave me time to pick berries and mushrooms for our soup.

We began to make a norm so everyone in the brigade received better wages. The Russians seemed impressed.

New Soviet Commissars came to our camp. The Commandant brought them to see our brigade to show how well we were producing. They needed to write a story; tell the world how well the expelled Poles were adapting to Russian life.

"How much work do you do? Can you do more? Is your life good here?" They peppered us with so many questions that we couldn't get a word in.

Then they let slip a bit of information. "You should be happy. The Germans have occupied your town. They're expelling everyone."

When they allowed me to talk, I showed them my hut. "Yes, we make our norm but never in our 8 hours. I sleep here to get more work done." (Okay. So I didn't tell him the type of extra work I did.)

I showed him the bread and mushroom soup (the mushrooms we picked in the forest) we were having and said, "How much longer can we work on food like this? In the bush, we can only buy one bowl of soup a day. And we can't afford to buy it every day."

Later that afternoon, the Commissars came to the bush cafeteria to eat with us. We were the first in line for the soup. The Commissars went first and the Russian cook gave them the noodles from the bottom of the pot. We came next and she took the water from the top for us.

My father showed this to the Commissars and said, "This is how the Soviet system works. We all were fed from the same pot. But you have a bowl full of noodles and we have a bowl full of water."

The Commissars stood up quickly and left without saying a word. We went back to work.

The Commissars left the camp. The Commandant called me in immediately. "How much bread do you need to be happy?"

"It's not how much bread we need. We need other things too. In 2 years you haven't brought us any meat. The only meat or even potatoes we got is what we traded for. How long can we survive without any real food?"

There were other camps, throughout the Soviet Union, that were far worse than our camp. You could always hear the jokes about Russian dissidents being sent to the salt mines; camps from which no one ever returned alive. Unfortunately, these stories were often true. There were salt mines but there were also mines that produced coal and iron and gold and the highly secret uranium. There were lead mines where every worker, entering, would soon die of lead poisoning.

All these mines needed a constant stream of new "workers". Every camp, in Russia, was expected to send men to these mines. Our camp would be no different.

Each Commandant had his own way of choosing the men to send away.

It was a Sunday, like any other, when the Russians brought in a large supply of vodka. There was going to be a celebration for no particular reason. They were to sell us as much as we wanted for just a token cost.

That was some night.

The next morning over 30 men were too hung over to report for work. By the time that we returned from work, that evening, these men had already been removed, taken to those camps, never to be seen again.

At times, new 'guests of the Soviet Union' would be brought to our camp. One such woman noticed the anti-social Ukrainians and began screaming.

"Murderers! Butchers!" She yelled.

We calmed her down and she told us her story. These Ukrainians had lived near her village. They knew the forests of the area. When the Russians came, they offered to lead the men of her family to safety, for a price. Her family accepted the offer but, a short time later, were found not far away in the bush; murdered.

We took her to the Commandant with her story. We wanted something done. At least have these men charged. The Commandant said that he didn't have the authority to charge them. They would be left alone.

When we would be freed from Siberia, the girls of this family wanted to go with us. Their father and brothers, obviously, wouldn't allow this. They remained to live, and hopefully to die, in this

Chapter Five – MAY 1941 – BRICKS

The Russians had decided that we were to remain here and start another village with no name. They marked off a series of lots, one of which would be given to each family. We were to clear the land and build homes for ourselves so that we would no longer have to live in the barracks.

One family had already begun to clear their lot near the bridge. I came upon two men looking at the ground, checking out the soil.

"Look at this soil. We haven't seen anything this good in all of Poland." I was told.

The two men, Bojairski and Kosierb, had been brick makers in Poland. They had owned a factory with twelve ovens. They told me that they could make excellent bricks using this Siberian clay.

As we talked, more men joined us. Everyone had his own area of expertise and we began wondering if we could do something with the materials that we had at hand. Each person came up with his own idea as we kept talking.

The Russians, always suspicious of us in a group, quickly told the Commandant that the men were gathering. In no time at all, he was there with us. He asked me what was going on.

I told him everything. By this time, we had decided that we had all the raw materials necessary to produce top quality bricks. Now we wanted to know if we could get official permission to start a brick factory.

The Commandant promised to ask his superiors and then broke up our meeting, sending us back to work.

About ten days later, the Commandant called me to his office again. The answer was "Yes". We had permission to produce bricks if we could do it with local materials; nothing would be imported, and if we had the expertise to do it on our own.

I assured him that we had two men who knew all about the manufacture of bricks. And we had several others who knew how to work with bricks, including myself. I had never worked with bricks before but figured that I could learn if I had to.

Bojairski and Kosierb determined how everything was to work. We started by digging large trenches, deep into the soil. They also had us make wooden moulds that would be used to form the bricks.

Not far from our camp, was another camp similar to ours. But they had a sawmill that they used to make lumber from the trees they cut. The good lumber was shipped out but the sides were left behind. Each of these sides consisted of the tree's outer trunk and the flat sawn side. We used this lumber to make tables to work on as well as platforms, on the ground, that would hold the raw bricks.

We began to work but immediately had a major problem. We didn't have enough water.

There was water, in the stream, just below us but we had no way of getting it to where we were mixing it with the soil. A man with a horse would bring one barrel at a time from the stream to the camp. He couldn't bring any extra for us.

So I volunteered, "If you give me two pails, I can carry the water up the bank from the stream." It was a steep climb but only a few hundred feet.

The Commandant was skeptical that this plan could work but allowed me to try.

He was right to be skeptical. It was hard to bring up enough water when it was needed.

On to plan "B".

The Russians occasionally shipped fish heads, for our soup, in barrels. Several barrels were left behind and were good enough to hold water. We gathered 20 barrels and I began to fill them with water. It was thus available whenever the workers needed it.

It was still hard climbing up the bank from the stream. So I cut 23 steps into the bank to make it easier to climb. At the bottom, I made a small platform into the stream. I made a yoke, to put on top of my shoulders, and hung a pail at each end. Now I could dip each pail into the stream, fill them with water, carry them up the bank and empty them into the barrels without removing either pail from the yoke.

We now had a plan. This could work. I asked the Commandant how much I would be paid to provide a constant supply of water.

We agreed on 10 kopecks per pail of water.

Now we began to work.

This was going to be hard work. Men dug out the soil and mixed it with water. When it was the proper consistency, it was shoveled into the moulds and tamped on the tables until each brick was solid. Each brick was then placed on the platform to dry in the sun.

All day long I carried water. When everyone else finished working, for the day, I continued carrying water until every barrel was full. This way, they could start the complete operation first thing in the morning. Every day I had to carry between 300 - 350 pails of water; 150 - 175 trips to the stream and back.

In less than two weeks, we had 10,000 bricks ready to be fired. We were ready to start the fire.

At the same time, the men had been digging four trenches. Each trench would be two meters wide and three meters deep. At one end, they dug out a fire-pit that was at least twice as wide as the rest of the trench. This system of trenches, in turn, was enclosed in a shack made with the rough lumber. We had to keep any wind and moisture away from the bricks while they were being cured.

Bojairski and Kosierb supervised the men as they placed the bricks into the trenches. First, the bricks were placed on the floor and against the walls. They then made a maze of bricks within each trench so that 2,500 bricks were placed into each trench. Finally, boards were placed over top of each trench to fully enclose each makeshift furnace. It took a good part of a week to arrange all the bricks properly.

Firewood was placed into each fire-pit and lit. We built up the fire and kept it burning day and night for two weeks. It took another week for the bricks to cool and another week to remove them from the trenches. They were dark black; the best bricks that any of us had ever seen.

We were paid at the end of each month. After the first month, of carrying water, I was to receive 900 Rubbles. That was four times as much as I would get for cutting trees in the bush.

The Commandant thought that this was too much to pay any one man. So I told him, "Find out what other camps would pay for a cubic meter of water and you can pay me the same amount."

It turned out that I would be paid even more if he would pay me the accepted rate that other camps paid. I simply reminded him that I worked well after everyone else had finished for the day. He still seemed to want to keep me away from other men when we weren't working. I kept this job, at 900 Rubbles per month for the rest of the summer.

Chapter Six – September 1941

The Russians were losing their war with Germany. Losing badly. Millions of men were being killed, taken prisoner or deserting. They desperately needed allies and troops. They hoped that they could use us.

The Polish government had established itself in exile, in London. The Russians signed a treaty with this government to fight the Germans. This treaty set free all the "special guests" the Russians had scattered throughout the Soviet Union.

It was Sept. 22 when more Commissars came to our camp. We were told to gather in the clearing before we went to work. They had good news for us, we were told. They liked how well we had adapted to our new lives. Of all the new settlements that they had created, this was one of the most successful. But none of us had built a new house so they offered us help. This would become a model community.

And the best news of all... They had brought, with them, citizenship papers for all of us. All we had to do was sign these papers and we would become citizens of the Soviet Union with all the rights of Soviet citizenship. In return, they wanted something from us.

We were told that the Soviet Union and Poland were allies again. The Russians were forming a Polish army on Soviet soil. This army would fight alongside their new Russian friends. They just needed us to volunteer for this new force.

One by one, we picked up our tools; axes, saws, shovels, my pails; and went back to work. Not one person accepted their offer. Not one person chose to be a Soviet citizen.

A few days later, Kosierb's daughter appeared in our camp looking for her father. "You are free." She told us. "We are all free."

She had a cousin who was now an ambassador in Moscow and used him to find her family.

She told us about the rest of the treaty that our government had signed. She told us that we were free to go wherever we wanted. But we still didn't know where we could go. After all, our homes were under German occupation.

That's when my cousin appeared. I hadn't seen him since his family had been separated from us when we were first reached Pinyug. My uncle had sent him to find us.

"A free Polish army is being formed in a place called Buzuluk." He told us. "Everyone is leaving; heading south."

Now we had a destination. Buzuluk, we discovered, was about 1,000 km. southeast of us, just north of the Kazakhstan Republic. The entire camp, with the exception of the Ukrainian murderers, would leave and head south. The Ukrainian girls wanted to go so badly but their fathers and brothers grabbed them and kept them from leaving.

We left our work and began preparing for this next journey. We left the bricks in the ovens and along with another 20,000 bricks that had been prepared to be fired in the winter.

The Commissars came to me one more time. "We are forming a Polish army." One of them repeated. "Convince the people to stay and we'll send you for officer training."

Those men who joined the Russians as a part of this Polish army would be used as cannon fodder amassing huge casualties.

I kept preparing to leave. My father had planted potatoes so we harvested them now. We gathered 15 bags of fresh potatoes to take with us. We killed our goat, bought a sheep and prepared the meat with the salt that we still had. My mother had 2 bags of dried bread. Whenever we could buy extra bread, she would dry it the same way that we dried our bricks. Then we used it in our soups. Everyone took as much as they could carry. Together, as the first snow began falling, we headed for the train station at Pinyug. Then we waited.

The Commandant came to see me at the station. They still wanted us to stay. "You'll be made a general if you convince the people to stay. You'll be in charge of the Siberian arm of your army." He promised.

I knew how much a Soviet promise was worth so I kept waiting for a train out. Even if any of us believed them, no one wanted to stay here. We didn't know this yet, but the Soviets had murdered over 15,000 Polish officers that had been taken prisoner. They had destroyed all the Polish leadership. Now they needed it back. Even a corporal could now be seen as a military leader.

We kept waiting at the station. Buzuluk was only 4 days south, by train. We had been waiting for 3 days here already. The station manager said there was no way that all of us could leave. The trains were crowded so we would have to leave in groups of 2 or 3, unless we were willing to lease entire cars. We needed 11 cars to carry all the people at once. Finally, we agreed to pay 300 rubbles per car to get a train that would take us south to where the Polish army was being formed.

Those of us, who had saved some money, paid for the cars. We loaded what few possessions and food that we had left and we were off.

We traveled south only a short distance before we reached the station at Kirov. This was the end of the line, we were told, and we were ordered off the train. We refused to move. There were already thousands of other people waiting at the station, waiting for a train to take them south. If we got off, we would just be more bodies in a mob of refugees.

We informed the officials that we had paid for these cars. They, eventually, did get new railway cars for us and we headed south. Slowly. We traveled south for another 6 days. At a large station several Polish soldiers in uniform met us. These were the first real Polish soldiers we had seen since being deported. It should have been a good sign for us.

No trains were being allowed into Buzuluk. It was already full of refugees, all of them as weak or even weaker than we were. And disease was taking its toll. These people had no resistance left and they were dying by the thousands. The officials couldn't cope with any more refugees.

Our train was being diverted to Samarkand, Tajikistan. This was twice as far from Buzuluk as Buzuluk was from Pinyug. There was no way that we were prepared for a trip of this length.

We had expected to travel for no more than a week and didn't have enough food for a trip of this duration. We shared our food with those people who didn't have enough and now had almost run out. The Polish soldiers gave us soup and bread but didn't have enough to give us any extra for the next leg of our journey. The Russians didn't want so many of their "special guests" to leave them and refused to supply us, soldiers or civilians with food.

Not everyone was willing to go on if we weren't assured of getting food. At the station, a local official said that we could stay at an area collective farm if we wanted. The Russians were taking as many men as possible for their army. The collective needed people, men or women, to replace them. A few Ukrainian families decided it would be safer to stay here and they left.

By trading with the people of the village with no name; by finding fields of cranberries and blueberries; by taking the initiative to make more money we survived our captivity in Siberia. In other such camps, hundreds of thousands of Poles had died. Finally, on this train trip, our people began dying. As we kept traveling, almost entirely without food, more families left us to go to the collectives.

At one stop we met Stefan Puka. He was little more than skin and bones. He begged me to take him with us. We didn't have enough food but he just kept pleading with me. He was alone, no one to watch over him. We couldn't leave him so we agreed to take him in our car.

On the journey, I learned his story. It was very similar to our own. He had been rounded up by the Soviets and sent by train to Siberia. There was a good chance that he passed through Pinyug after we had arrived. But they kept moving him northward. He eventually ended up on the island of Novaya Zemlya, which separated the Barents Sea and the Kara Sea, well north of the Arctic Circle where he had to work at a gold mine.

This was one of the camps where the Russians sent people, knowing that they wouldn't survive for long: a death camp. Stefan was young and strong so he lasted longer than most of the men there. They had no villagers to trade with and no crops of berries with which to supplement their meals. They had to die.

Stefan was still alive when the Russians agreed to free us. The men at

Novaya Zemlya were given the same opportunity as we were given: sign the citizenship papers and get all the rights of Soviet citizens. Again, no one accepted the deal. Therefore, the Russians agreed to bring all the surviving men to Arkhangel'sk to be sent back south.

The Russians brought 3 ships to the island. They loaded all the survivors into the holds, locked the doors and headed to the mainland. Late into the night, as most of the men slept, the ships became quiet and stopped.

Once the men freed themselves, they discovered that they were alone. The crews had abandoned all 3 ships. There was no fuel or food left behind. They had been left to die.

The ships were anchored in the White Sea, in view of the Russian shoreline. The men had few options. Either die on the ships or try to swim to land. Swim in Arctic water in September. They rounded up anything that could float and threw it into the sea. Then they jumped in.

Stefan and 2 other men grabbed onto a wooden table and started swimming towards shore. Stefan was the only one to make it. A peasant found him, as much dead as alive, and took him home where his family nursed Stefan back to health. But they were afraid of the Russian authorities. As soon as he was well enough to walk, they told him to leave. He took the trains south until he met us.

Stefan Puka would die in battle, in Italy.

We continued traveling. We would move by night but every day we would be parked on a side railing or station. At one station, another train had been stopped ahead of us. When we went near it, the stench was unbearable. We watched as they opened the cars and started pushing the men out. They were skeletons. Many could hardly move and the soldiers kicked them until everyone was out. We weren't allowed to get near them. These men were prisoners. Most likely they were political prisoners who the Soviets didn't want to fall into German hands. They put the men on trains and moved them east like all the machinery from their factories. They fed them as well as they fed the machines.

We finally arrived in Samarkand, Uzbekistan. Of all the people who, started with us in Pinyug, only half remained. The rest had either died or stayed at various collectives along our route.

From the station, we walked into a bazaar where the Uzbeks couldn't help but notice the strangers. Once they discovered that we were Polish, they became excited. They wanted to trade for anything that had a symbol of Poland on it; Polish money if we had it.

A large crowd gathered around us. The men, in broken Russian, began telling us their story.

This was the land of the Tatars who were once fierce warriors. Their ancestors, under the leadership of Genghis Khan, conquered large territories in Asia. In 1241 they attacked Europe. Their armies made it to the walls of Krakow.

They attacked during Easter Mass. A trumpeter, in a watchtower, sounded the alarm but an arrow hit him in the throat. He was killed in the middle of his call to arms. The people of Krakow heard the alarm. They manned the rampart and fought the Tatars. The countryside was looted but the fortress remained unconquered.

A Tatar prophet blamed the defeat on the fact that the troops attacked during such a holy day. He said that this meant their empire would be destroyed. It was an archer from Samarkand who fired that first shot. All the Tatar people would be enslaved until a Polish trumpeter came to Samarkand and finished playing the tune that the original trumpeter had tried playing those many centuries ago.

They asked us if we could do this for them. Asked us to lift the curse and help restore their freedom.

I knew that we had a trumpeter with us. We brought him to the bazaar and, in front of a gathering crowd, he played the anthem "The Krakow Hejnal" from start to finish. The people cheered. They knew their days of enslavement were ending. It may take a generation or two but they knew they would finally throw out their Russian masters and regain their own nation. It was just a matter of time before the Soviet Union would disintegrate. And it all started that day.

Another morning we woke up to discover that our train was stopped at the end of the line. Literally. We were in the middle of a field on a dead end track. The engine had left us there.

We could tell that this was good farmland even though the crops had been harvested. The harvesters must have been careless. We found large heads of millet lying on the ground throughout the field. Everyone grabbed any type of bag they could find and started gathering the leftover grain. We filled the 3 bags in which we had brought our potatoes. Other people filled pillowcases with grain. Men took off their shirts and packed as much grain into them as they could.

Just over a kilometer away, was the collective that worked these fields. Several people went there to try and trade for potatoes.

There was no water here. We chewed the millet but we weren't able to make any soup from it yet.

They left us here for 2 days. On the second night, while we slept, the engine came back. We were being moved again. 8 families were left behind, either because they wanted to stay or because they weren't expecting the train.

Traveling another day and 2 nights we finally reached a large city. They backed our cars into a station and simply left us. This was Tashkent. We were finally able to get some water and make ourselves a meal of soup. We were given nothing else to eat.

The next place they took us was Czyrakezi. They unhooked and left 3 cars, including our car, at the station and took the other 4 cars further. They would go on to Ashabet, which is next to the border of Afghanistan.

We called out for bread. The station Commandant told the peasants to bring us food. What we got was the millet pancakes that were the staple food of the region.

The entire station was in ruins. All the buildings had been knocked down as if by an earthquake. I asked the Commandant if I could work for him, repairing the station, in return for food. He agreed, so John Grzejoczyk and I began by cleaning all the debris from his office.

This town had a factory for cleaning and preparing cotton that was being grown in this region. Every day, all day, caravans of camels came to the factories. Each camel carried 2 huge bags of raw cotton.

Even with these cotton factories, there was no work for our families. And the Soviets insisted that we work. Donkey carts, driven by Uzbeks, were brought to the station. We were being taken to a town called Chartarczi where we would be put to work. I stayed behind to work on the station.

It was only 4 days, after our people were taken, that Eddie came back. Our family didn't stay in Chartarczi but were taken to a Collective in the mountains. "You have to come with me," he pleaded. "They've put us in a stable and refuse to feed us. They put us there to die."

I left work immediately, without getting any food or pay. We walked all night. The next day we found a shack and some water and rested for an hour. We walked all day and into the next night. There was only one road running into the mountains so we couldn't miss the Collective even at night.

When we reached the Collective that night, the people were having a celebration, sitting on carpets around a huge fire.

No one seemed able to speak Russian but I managed to get some food. We were brought bowls of rice in sheep fat. No matter how hungry we were, this was all but impossible to eat.

The next morning, I saw the hovel in which we were supposed to live. It had once been a stable. Now it wasn't good enough for their animals. It was 4 walls on a dirt floor with no roof or door. My father took me to the Commander, of the Collective, who spoke Russian.

I started yelling. "I'm going to call the authorities. We came here as free people not as prisoners. We are here to form an army."

He finally gave us the meat of an old sheep. We pulled up some dry weeds and used them to make a fire. Mother made us soup of the old sheep and the millet we had gathered.

Not far away, I saw tractors plowing a field. We went to talk to the men. The workers were Russian. They shared some of their tea and millet cakes as we talked.

There was a larger settlement nearby. We discovered that they needed a blacksmith. Father agreed to go and work for them.

It was now early December and a cold rain came.

We had to find cover from the rain. I chopped down a few poplar trees and used them to make a frame for a roof. The Uzbeks showed me how to put on a sod roof. And we were able to close in our quarters.

10 days after he left, father came back to us. He was weaker then the last time we saw him. He had been worked but wasn't given any food or pay. The trains were leaving again, he told us.

We hurried back to Czyrakezi to find that all the other families were already there, also expecting to leave. All of our 7 cars were joined again and we went back the way we came. We stopped at a station in Zerbulock.

There, waiting for us, were more carts driven by Kazaks. 1 or 2 families were placed into each cart and we were gone.

Our family was put in a cart with 4 members of the Kufel family. Stefan Puka also came with us.

It was night when we reached another Collective and we were told to go into a building. It was another stable, much like our previous "home". There was no light of any sort so we felt along the walls and eventually went to sleep on the floor.

When morning came, we discovered that this stable was indeed like the last one. Again, it was 4 walls with no door, no windows, a dirt floor and no roof. Again we had to find the Commander in order to get some pancakes for breakfast. He told us that we would have to work as long as we stayed there. In return we would get 1/2 kg. of millet.

This Collective grew cotton and raised sheep. The cotton had been harvested and we were to clear the fields of the cotton stems. We did. We pulled enough stems each day to set on fire to keep ourselves warm and cook our meals.

Through the fields, there were canals that carried water to irrigate each year's cotton crop. Along the canals, there grew rushes, poplars and plum trees. The plums had been picked long ago but I took my axe and cut some dead wood so we could make a better fire. We gathered the rushes and made mats from them. Now we had something, other than a dirt floor, to sleep on. Along some canals, we found wild onions and garlic. No one else seemed to want them so we gathered what we could to add flavor to our soup.

This is when I found an old building hidden among the trees. It had fallen long ago but I thought the metal from the roof and the bricks that made up the walls could be useful.

The metal made a good roof for our shack. Father also used it to make us a door. We brought the bricks back and used them to make ourselves a stove and chimney inside our shack.

The Commander saw our stove and new door and wanted the same for his house. I built him a stove and father made him a new door.

Then he asked us to make a larger stove for the washroom. The men would heat stones on the stove and put them into a pail of water. Then they would use the steam to help shave themselves. For all this work, the Commander gave us a 10 kg. bag of dried plums.

On December 11, while we were somewhere in southern Russia, the Japanese attacked Pearl Harbor. That act was going to change the war again, but not for us. Not yet.

The Polish army was being formed and most of the young men were volunteering. Eddie, a Kufel boy and Stefan Puka left to join the army. I stayed because my family needed me here more.

One day, while the men were out in the fields, the Collective's sheep were spooked and started to run. They ran past the houses and one of the sheep ran right through our open door — right into my mother.

I had left my axe behind so mother grabbed it and, with every ounce of strength she could muster, smashed it against the sheep's head. Killing it. Quickly, she wrapped it in our mats and put it in the far corner. Then she lay down next to it. When an Uzbek came looking for any lost sheep, all he found was an old woman sleeping.

When father came back, he cleaned the sheep but he was afraid that we might not be able to eat it. What would these people do if they knew that we had killed one of their sheep?

There was a village market not far from this Collective. This gave father an idea. He went to the market and bought an old sheep. A very cheap old sheep. He brought it back and killed it in front of our shack so that everyone saw it. Now everyone knew that we had meat for our family. We could cook the meat of the young sheep and people would think we were eating old mutton.

Diseases that had stopped us from going to Buzuluk were spreading. Everywhere, there were lice and fleas that carried disease from one camp to another. Finally, my mother became very sick.

We called the lone doctor from the village. He simply looked at her from outside the shack and pronounced, "She has typhoid fever."

It was a serious disease but he had an offer for us. He would give us the medicines we needed to care for her under one condition. He had noticed that my father had a gold bridge for his teeth. "Give me your gold. I'll make you a metal replacement and give you the medicine."

My father was in no condition to go through an operation of this sort even if we could trust the doctor. He let us know that he would not help us.

We had one choice left. Go to the market and try to trade for enough money to buy some medicine. We had one treasure left.

Just before the war, my sister Sophie received a new coat for her birthday. A very beautiful coat that cost of 700 Zloti, the equivalent of $150. She took it from home and never wore it. She would only wear it once we were home again. This was the one item we could not lose.

Until now.

Father took the coat to the market. Maybe he could get enough for it to supply us with money for the next few months.

As soon as he reached the market and brought out the coat, a woman came up to him. She was the Jewish woman who owned the general store. Everyone could see that she wanted the coat.

She asked father why he wanted to sell it. He told her that he needed some medicine.

"Oh how unfortunate," she said. "I happen to own the only drug store here. Maybe, I can help you."

"Would you buy this coat?" He asked.

"Oh no! No. Why would I want a fancy coat like that? Where could I possibly wear it?"

So father told her that he would sell something and come to her with the money.

"Oh no! No." she said. "I don't want your money. But I will trade you some medicines for your coat."

She offered him some aspirin, iron tonic and a disinfectant in exchange for the coat. These were worth a few rubbles. Maybe one or two Zloti. That wasn't enough, he told her.

"It's the coat for the medicine. Or you will get nothing. Not in this village."

Finally, father walked away with the aspirin, the tonic and the disinfectant and she tried on her war booty.

We shaved my mother, washed her with the disinfectant and gave her the tonic and aspirin for the pain. She started getting better.

That's when the bad news started. Mrs. Shikora, who had been with us in Pinyug, came to see us. "I'm so sorry to tell you but Eddie died. He caught the typhoid. I saw them taking his body from the hospital."

We were all shocked. We never expected this. They should have medication and doctors, at the army base, to treat typhoid. I had to go and see for myself.

Then father got sick.

We didn't have any medicines left for him and we couldn't get any more. The doctor wanted to take him to the hospital but we preferred to keep him with us. But the doctor convinced the camp Commander that he shouldn't have anyone infected with typhoid at the Collective.

The Commander ordered that he be taken to the hospital.

Late the next day, once I felt my mother would be fine, I went to see about my father. I found the hospital but no one was there. The doors were locked and iron bars sealed all the windows.

I yelled. From inside, I heard my father. He was crying in pain as he called back to me. "They've electrocuted me! Knocked me unconscious! They pulled out my teeth for the gold! Help me!"

I couldn't get in. I had to go back for help. I begged him to hold on and left. I came back with my axe and pry bars to open the hospital and with a cart to take my father back with me.

Once I broke into the hospital, I couldn't find anyone. It was empty. An Uzbek had driven me here in his cart. Now he came to me. He took me to a shed behind the hospital.

There, alone, in the middle of the shed lay my father.

Naked!

Dead!

Chapter Seven – SPRING, 1942

By the spring of 1942, the invading Axis armies were being brought to a halt. In the Pacific, the Japanese were in complete control. But, on April 18, sixteen American B-25 bombers under the command of Colonel James Doolittle bombed several cities on mainland Japan. This caused the Japanese leadership to stop the expansion of their empire and to consolidate their holdings.

The Germans had taken all of Poland from their Russians allies but were stopped short of Leningrad in the north and Moscow in the center. They continued a slow advance towards Stalingrad in the south. Thousands of Russian soldiers were being killed. Hundreds of thousands continued surrendering to the Germans.

I went to find the police officer, for the town, and report my father's murder. I kept trying to explain what had happened but he just kept saying, "I don't understand Russian."

Finally, he gave up. "It doesn't matter what he did to you." The officer said. "He is our doctor." And he walked away.

That was it. There was a new graveyard not far from the hospital. There were hundreds of freshly dug graves. I added one more grave to the cemetery. I buried my father on March 31, 1942.

There was little time for grieving. I had to find out what had happened to Eddie. I sold my army boots and took a job loading wood onto camels. This gave me enough money to buy some bread to leave with my family while I was gone.

Every train, that passed this area, would stop at Zerbulock's station to take on water. Leaving the station, to get back on the main track, the trains would have to move slowly along a sharp curve. I needed to get aboard one of these trains but didn't have enough money to waste on a ticket.

I waited until night. As the train slowed, on its way out, I ran along side and grabbed one of the cars. I held on in the dark and would eventually go inside. This way I could get a free ride all the way to Kirmeneh.

The Polish army had its encampment about 15 km. from the station at Kirmeneh. I had no way to get there other than to walk. I had made it half way when I saw 3 army trucks coming towards me. Standing on the road, I waved to stop them.

"I'm looking for my brother, Eddie Dobrucki." I called to the men in the first truck. "Do you know him?"

A soldier called back, "Yes. He's in the last truck."

And they were off. I had to turn around and walk back the way I came.

Finally, back at Kirmeneh, I found Eddie. Yes, he had been sick with Typhus and had been taken from the hospital. Whereas, most men who were that sick died, he had survived. Now he was being sent to Persia.

The whole unit was leaving in 2 days. If I could get everyone here by that time, we could all go with them. But it had taken me almost 2 days to get here. It would take another 2 days to get back to our family.

When I got back to Zerbulock, we gathered everything that we had left; sheets, clothes, and even my 2 pails from Siberia; and headed for the station. I knew that, even though I could hop the train, the rest of the family couldn't. So, I had to get some tickets. Real tickets.

The Kufel family was still with us. They wanted to go with us. Their son was also in the army, and was being shipped to Persia along with Eddie. Unfortunately, I didn't have enough money for all of us to ride to Kirmeneh.

The station was crowded with people trying to be anywhere but here. Every train, leaving, was leaving fully loaded. My Polish army uniform was still mostly intact, except for my boots, which I had to sell. I put on my uniform and my Siberian shoes, hoping that no one would notice, and stormed to the ticket counter.

"I need 20 tickets for Kirmeneh, for the army." I demanded.

"No. We don't have any." The ticket agent answered.

But, since it was for the army, she gave me 4 tickets. At least this was a beginning. And I didn't have to pay for them.

Back with my family, I prepared to get them on the train. I was going to try to get my mother, 2 brothers, 2 sisters and the 3 Kufels on the train with only 4 tickets. As for myself, I was going to stay behind for now.

I had a little money left over so I gave a few rubbles to each person just in case one person might get robbed while on the train. Then, all together, we went forward to try and board the train.

The conductor stopped us as we began boarding. He saw that we had only 4 tickets and wouldn't let anyone on. Then he saw the 30 rubbles that I had given Sophie, in her hand. Most likely, he was accustomed to taking small bribes in return for a place on the train. He grabbed the 30 rubbles and pushed everyone else aside. All of our 8 persons got onto the train.

Later that night, I took as much of our possessions as I could carry and jumped another train. We arrived, far too late, at Kirmeneh. The Polish army had left and we were stranded. The camp, where the army had stayed, was now abandoned. But they had left behind some tents. Refugees had begun to settle in that camp. We joined them.

That night, I again jumped the train to return and get the rest of our possessions. I had left these possessions with another family that I knew. Once again, I went to the ticket office in my army uniform. Again, I was given a few tickets. I picked up the last of our possessions and, with the people who had watched them, left for good.

My mother was waiting for me at our new camp. "Try this." She said, handing me a piece of cooked meat. "What do you think of it? What do you think it is?"

It was meat. That's all I could tell. I had no idea what sort of beast it could have come from. Turns out it was turtle. There were a lot of turtles in the area, at first, and they were easy to catch.

Eventually, 600 Polish refugees called this camp "home". Whatever authorities were in charge of this camp would give us a bit of flour every other day. We would add a little turtle meat and some grass to the flour and make a sort of soup. Rye grass and clover were the best as long as you didn't eat too much of the clover grass. Eating too much would give you diarrhea. If we couldn't find these, any type of grass would do. We would pull out any grass, we could find, roots and all.

The turtles, though easy to catch, were difficult to kill. They would hide within their shells to stay safe. The trick was to get them out of their shells. All you needed was a fire and an axe. You put the turtle over the fire. To try and get away, it would have to put out its head. That's where the axe came into play.

Wood was hard to find. But once the turtle shells dried in the sun, they could be used as firewood.

If we were lucky enough to catch a female turtle, she would often times still have some eggs inside her. The yolks would cook up well but the whites wouldn't. They remained sloppy, rubber-like ooze but at least they were edible — barely edible.

As the months went on, it was harder to find food. I would go into the mountains with my axe and a sack. I would search for the occasional turtle or just some young grasses. The Uzbek farmers would also take their sheep into the mountains so good grass was hard to find.

One day, while hunting the elusive turtle, from nowhere a sheep ran up to me. Seconds later, it was dead and in my sack, heading back to our camp. This sheep was different than any sheep I had seen before. It didn't have much meat but it did have large amounts of fat on its hindquarters. It provided us with some meat and 2 full pails of fat.

Another day, in late summer, I found a field where the wheat had just been cut. The sheaves of wheat were piled into stacks to dry. I began tearing off the heads from the sheaves and filling my sack. I didn't hear the horses until 2 Uzbeks grabbed me.

I was too weak to fight and ready to give up the grain that I had taken. I put my hand into the sack and tried to make it known that they could have their grain back. But one Uzbek grabbed the sack and pulled it away from me. That's when they first saw the axe in my hand. They stood for a moment, staring at me, then jumped back on their horses and galloped away.

I had no idea if they were coming back so I grabbed what grain I had and ran the other way.

We stayed in this camp through the summer and into the fall. Some of the children were gradually being evacuated. Bolek and Dolek were evacuated that summer. They would start on a new adventure of their own. The Polish army was looking for young recruits. They were still only 15 years old, which was one year too young to join the forces. But, since no one had any papers, our mother told the recruiter that the boys were 16 years old, just small for their age.

The recruits were marched out in the middle of the night, put on a train, then a ship and finally ended up in Tehran. There they spent the next few months in school finishing grade 5. Then they were trucked to Palestine to join 1,200 other teens.

In Palestine Bolek and Dolek were met by recruiters who wanted trainees to attend the RAF Technical school. They were among 300 recruits to be chosen to train for the air force and shipped to England.

It was November 22 when, finally, the rest of us were to be moved out. There were only about 200 of us left alive. And we were all weak and malnourished. We were put on wagons and driven west to the Caspian Sea port of Krasnovodsk.

It was a dirty town. A pipeline brought oil to Krasnovodsk where it was loaded aboard tankers and shipped out. It was obvious that no one cared about the environment. The entire shore was covered in oil. Every step we took, we stepped in oil soaked sand.

We hadn't been given any water since we left our camp. Now we were being taken aboard an oil tanker. Our mother was too weak to walk so we had to carry her aboard on our last remaining bed spread. We put her beneath some stairs to try and shield her from the sun. Then I went looking for water. An Uzbek let me know that he would trade for my army belt. I gave him my belt and he gave me 2 bottles of wine. It wasn't water but it would do.

They left us all above deck, in the open. We sailed due south until the far shore became visible. And then we stopped. This could be the same thing that happened to Stefan Puka on the White Sea, we thought. The Russians might simply leave us here to die. But, eventually, small boats came to the tanker to take us to shore. We left several more people, dead, on the tanker.

They left us on the beach and we began walking as well as we could. We were more dead than alive. Coming towards us, we saw a vision. A young girl in a white robe. We didn't know if it was a hallucination or something real. Not until we heard her crying as she watched almost 200 living skeletons coming towards her.

I knew this girl. It was Mary Bema. Aniela, her older sister, for a short time, had been in my brigade, in Pinyug. Crying, she gave out bread and dates.

"Don't eat too much." She warned. "Just a little or you'll get sick. You'll have food here. All you need."

We would survive.

Chapter Eight – Back to the War

Just south of the Caspian Sea, around Tehran, the British had established resettlement camps for anyone who could escape the Soviet Union. We would be among the last people that the Russians would allow to leave.

General Wladyslaw Anders had been appointed commander of all Polish forces in Russia. He kept pressing the Allies to force the Russians to allow all Polish citizens, regardless of ethnicity, to be allowed to leave. Stalin refused to allow out ethnic Ukrainians or Byelorussians even if they were Polish citizens. As sort of a concession, they did allow 4,000 Poles of Jewish religion - but only if they had family members in the Polish army - to leave.

True to Mary Bema's word, we had enough food and care to regain our health. From this camp, as well as other refugee camps established in the region, people would be organized to be transported to other British territories to wait out the war.

My mother, Sophie and Loni were sent to Palestine and would later be sent to England to rejoin Bolek and Dolek. There were thousands of children left orphaned. They would be sent to camps in India, Uganda and South Africa.

I spent two weeks in this camp before I rejoined the army. I was assigned to an artillery unit. Finally, I was getting to use some modern equipment. I would be taught how to aim the guns. How to put the shells exactly where the spotters told me to put them. And then I would teach other crews how to do the same.

The Polish army was being reformed. We were again Polish soldiers under Polish command as a part of the British 8th Army. We continued training in Iran while at the same time guarding the oil fields that were so important to the war effort. No one knew if the Russians would prevent the Germans from breaking through their lines at Stalingrad and reaching the Middle East or if the Germans still had their own allies in this region.

Wasn't Iraq supposed to be a desert? Yes, we did face sandstorms. And yes, it was hot. But there was more. The rains came and came. It was hot and wet; the perfect weather for mosquitoes. So now we had to face a new disease. Malaria. And people kept dying.

One day a group of soldiers from one of our artillery supply units came upon Iranian peasants who had just killed a mother bear. The

Iranians were about to kill her lone cub when the soldiers stepped in. Having so many orphans around us, they felt a kinship with the small-orphaned cub. They bought him from the Iranians and named him Wojtek. The first part of his

name stood for, in Polish, warrior and the last half stood for joyful. For the remainder of the war, he became the mascot of the Polish artillery; each unit taking turns caring for him. For a time he lived in my tent.

Eventually, someone gave the bear some beer. It turned out that Wojtek liked beer. It got to the point that, when he wanted a drink, he would grab and hold up an artillery shell waiting to trade the shell for a beer. That is why the coat of arms of our artillery units was a bear, holding an artillery shell.

Wojtek would travel with us for the rest of the war. It was against regulations to take an animal into a war zone, even if that animal was your mascot. Therefore, Wojtek was enlisted into the Polish army, artillery division, and even received his own serial number.

Wojtek was a real soldier. During our battle at Monte Casino, he joined his fellow soldiers in carrying crates of shells from the trucks to the artillery guns. He never dropped a shell.

In the fall of 1943 the Russians began driving the Germans west. Once the oil fields were seen to be safe, our forces began moving to

Wojtek Soldier Bear

Insignia of Polish Artillery

Palestine. I was stationed in Gaza but did a lot of training in Lebanon and Syria. We learned how to take apart our guns and move them through the hills. The plan, at that time, was to attack Germany by going through Greece and the Balkans, which Churchill referred to as "the soft underbelly of the Axis".

In Palestine other Polish units joined us. Many soldiers, who had escaped during the early days of the war, ended up with the British in North Africa. They formed the Carpathian brigade and fought in the battles around Tobruk. German Field Marshal Rommel named them the "Desert Rats". Together we became the 2nd Polish Corps.

Stalin vetoed the Allied invasion through the Balkans. Under no circumstances did he want Allied troops conquering any territory in Central Europe, which he wanted to control. So we were moved across the Suez Canal into Egypt.

As we began moving from Palestine, soldiers began deserting. Three thousand trained and armed soldiers, of the Jewish faith, left the Polish army to join the Israeli settlement movement.

Even after living in Europe for hundreds of years and intermarrying throughout Europe, they still considered themselves to be Jewish. They didn't want to be a part of our war to free Poland because they never wanted Poland to be their home.

The British ordered General Anders to arrest all of them as deserters. Anders refused, saying, "They feel that they are now at home and want to fight for their own country."

One thousand soldiers of the Jewish faith remained with us. They were a part of us, we were a part of them and we wanted to fight, together, to free our homeland.

One of the soldiers who stayed in Palestine was a young corporal, Menachem Begin, who would later become Prime Minister of Israel.

The British and Americans attacked Italy through Sicily and the toe of the Italian boot. We began landing in Italy in Dec. 1943 and Jan. 1944 at Taranto on the heal of the Italian peninsula. Then we began moving north along the Adriatic coast.

The Allies were finally stopped south of Rome at the Gustav Line. This was a line of fortifications across the whole width of Italy. It was anchored along the western edge at Monte Casino. The monastery atop this mount was the main fort, the major defensive position. Hitler ordered that this line be held at all costs and sent his best-trained troops to hold it.

The British, Americans, Canadians, Indian, French and New Zealand troops attacked the monastery but were all repulsed, all with heavy casualties. The entire area was bombed to the point that the monastery was turned into rubble. This only helped to provide more defensive positions. Along with caves, trenches and concrete pillboxes behind miles of barbed wire and thousands of land mines, the Germans had a strong defensive position.

It was in Feb. of 1944 that Churchill admitted he had agreed that Stalin be allowed to keep all the land of Poland, Hitler had promised him. Stalin would be allowed to keep our homes.

It was shortly after this announcement that the Allies came to General Anders and asked him to send the Polish army against Monte Casino. There was a heated debate among the officers and men. We were fighting for our homeland. Why should we lose more men against an impregnable defense when we knew our hopes of going home had been betrayed?

General Anders made his decision. We would attack. Maybe this battle would bring out the point that we were still allies. Maybe it wasn't too late to change some minds. Maybe it wasn't too late to get our homes back.

It took 4 weeks to prepare for the attack. Our first battle was taking the town Venafro that is just west of Casino. While the infantry planned how they were going to get up the mountains, we began making bunkers for our artillery. We put up netting covered with grass and branches to camouflage our work and put heavy oak tree trunks in front of the heaviest guns. We could shoot over these trunks and we hoped that they would stop any return fire.

It was my job to get the direction and elevation for the guns and fire one, two but never more than three shots so that our spotters could mark where the shells would hit. Then we would move to another location to place more guns. We always moved at night so the Germans couldn't track us. The men would lead the way to check for land mines. They would place white towels behind their shoulders so that the man behind could see and follow. A truck, lights off and running as quietly as possible, would follow pulling our artillery.

The attack began at 11 p.m. on May 11. All the Allied guns opened up at once turning night into day. As our troops assaulted the monastery, American and British troops attacked other points along the Gustav Line.

The artillery bombardment didn't destroy the German positions. They had their own artillery and machine guns to hit back at us. And they were dug in on high ground. Our troops would attack and the Germans would counterattack. At one point, the Germans determined the position of our artillery and opened up with all their guns. The oak trunks, in front of us, were shredded and the bunker was blasted to pieces. My men and I had just left that position minutes earlier.

The Germans knew that it was the Polish army who was attacking and they aimed their loudspeakers and their propaganda at us. Whenever there was a lull in the fighting, they would tell us what gains the Russians were making going through Poland. And that we would have no place to return because our land was being given to the Russians.

Our troops kept attacking and being counterattacked. We kept moving forward; bringing in support staff to take the place of fallen soldiers.

The final attack came on May 18. At 10:20 a.m. a quickly made Polish flag was raised over the monastery. Then a bugle sounded. The sound of "the Krakow Hejnel" spread down over the troops.

We had lost over twelve hundred soldiers with another twenty eight hundred wounded in this battle. But the Gustav Line was broken and the Germans were fleeing. The American 5th Army had landed north of the line and now it was their job to close the escape route for the beaten, retreating Germans. But General Mark Clark saw Rome, with no Germans in sight, waiting to be "liberated". He marched his troops north to Rome, allowing tens of thousands of elite German soldiers a chance to retreat and reform and cause thousands more casualties among Allied troops.

June 6 was D-Day. Allied troops landed in Normandy. Eddie would land a few days later as part of the Polish Armored Division.

Again we were sent to fight our way up the Adriatic coast. On July 17 we attacked the port of Ancona. This was a major port and the Germans weren't going to give it up easily. Huge German cannons protected Ancona. These cannons had barrels that were large enough to allow a man to crawl into. Because they were so big, they were stationed on permanent concrete mounts.

Instead of hitting them head on, we moved all our men and artillery through the hills surrounding the Germans. All that practice we had moving artillery through the hills in Lebanon and Syria now paid off. We attacked on their sides with everything we had. The Germans were caught be surprise and they ran. And we chased them.

The Germans had troops carriers bringing reinforcements into Ancona. The retreating soldiers ran to the sea to try to get on board these ships and escape. With boats full of reinforcements and with all the fleeing soldiers, the whole port was in chaos. The British brought in their ships and their planes and they started shelling and bombing. The Germans surrendered to us on July 18.

Promotions were due. I was finally a sergeant.

On July 27 the Russians captured Lwow and our home. They continued west and reached the outskirts of Warsaw by Aug. 1. That's when the Polish Home Army began a full-scale military operation against the German Army expecting to be a part of the liberation of Warsaw. That's also when the Russians stopped advancing.

When the Home Army radioed for help, the Allies tried sending supplies from Italy. But the distance, plus having to fly over the Alps, allowed them to only send in small amounts of aid. The Americans tried flying aid from Britain but again it was too far to send any meaningful aid because the Russians refused to allow them to land in any area they controlled.

The Russians refused to give any sort of help. They wanted all Poles who could resist Communist occupation to be eradicated. And they saw nothing wrong with allowing the Germans to do it.

On Oct. 2 Warsaw again surrendered. This time with an additional 250,000 people dead. Hitler ordered the city to be destroyed so that "there is no where that one brick is sitting atop another brick".

After the battle for Ancona, we were sent south to Cvitanova Marche for rest and recuperation. The British Army went on to capture the port of Rimini. The Germans counterattacked in full force and our leave was cut short to stop the advance.

The rains came that fall and winter to Italy and refused to stop. Our final battle was to be the capture of Bologna. We prepared the attack in early Dec. and hoped to have it finished by Christmas. But the mud made movement of heavy equipment all but impossible. We waited for the rains to stop. But they didn't.

It wasn't until the spring, April 9, 1945 that we attacked in full force. We finally occupied Bologna on April 21.

On April 29, the German commander signed the unconditional surrender of all German troops in Italy. The end of all fighting would take place on May 2.

On April 30, Hitler committed suicide.

May 8 was V-E Day.

Chapter Nine – Decisions

Finally the war was over for us. We were in a foreign land while our homeland was still in turmoil after having two savage armies roll through it. No one knew what our next step would be.

But if we were to be stranded, it would be hard to find a better country than Italy in which to wait. Poland and Italy had a warm history uniting them for almost a thousand years. It began when Italian priests came to Poland to introduce the nation to Christianity. For the rest of their history, scholars, nobles, artists and priests would travel between the two countries. The people remained on friendly terms even while Austrian, German and Russian armies were occupying Poland.

Now we had tens of thousands of soldiers with nothing to do and not knowing where to do it. Our forces were moved to the port city of Ravenna to await further orders.

I was now fluent in Italian so I was made the liaison official between our troops and the citizens of Ravenna. The men needed to let off steam after years of facing death every day. The townspeople wanted to celebrate the end of the war in their part of the world. My job was to get these groups together without creating problems.

I set up a series of dances. The only way that a person was allowed into the hall was with a pass. Our men knew that they had to be well behaved if they were to get a pass. And once at the party, they were expected to be gentlemen.

We needed women of good character to come to these dances. I went into the city and met with officials to ensure them that anyone coming to these dances would be treated with respect. I went to churches and asked the priests to give out tickets to single women who they knew and respected. I went to city offices to find single women who were working for the city. And I asked about single women who were going to university.

These dances with good music, good food and an occasional bottle of good Italian wine brought our two groups together. Several hundred marriages would result from couples meeting here.

North of us, the map of Europe was changing. The Soviet Union was absorbing the Baltic Nations. The Eastern half of Poland, which Hitler had promised to Stalin, became a part of the Soviet Union. It was divided between the Belorussian and Ukrainian Soviet Socialist

Republics. The southern half of East Prussia and a slice of eastern Germany were added to Poland. The German citizens, from this area, were relocated into Soviet controlled Germany that became the nation of East Germany. Some ethnic Poles, who had remained in the part of Poland that the Soviet Union annexed, were moved to take the place of the Germans who were being removed. Other Poles would remain in their homes in what was now the expanded Soviet Union. They would never be treated as real citizens. Never be given the right to further education, government jobs or any type of support. Our homes were given to ethnic Ukrainian peasants and the ethnic Russians who would rule them.

The gulags of Siberia had been depopulated so hundreds of thousands of people from the new Poland were arrested. Once again they were put onto trains and deported to the work camps in Siberia. Any material goods that could be stolen were taken by the trainload, back to Russia.

And then there were the soldiers. Throughout the war, the Polish Home Army fought against both the German and Russian invaders. And both the Germans and the Russians simply killed any member of the Home Army that they caught. The exception was the thousands of soldiers who fought in the Warsaw uprising. When they surrendered to the Germans, they were treated as P.O.W.s and taken to prison camps in Germany.

The Russians wouldn't treat them the same way. Those men, and even women, who were freed from German P.O.W. camps, were seen as a threat. Any one who was seen as a threat to the newly appointed Russian puppet government was arrested. They demanded that the Allies return all the P.O.W.s that the Germans had captured in what was now Soviet occupied territory, back to the Soviets. 100,000 of these persons would be executed.

Our army was going to be decommissioned so the men had to decide where to go. Very few wanted to go back to what was left of Soviet occupied Poland. Especially those whose homes were now taken over by the Russians. Would we be sent back to Siberia?

Those soldiers who returned to Poland were treated as heroes, at first. But as the Russians put more loyal Communists in charge of the government, these returning soldiers were viewed suspiciously. After all, they had refused to fight in the Russian army and had instead joined with the British. They obviously couldn't be trusted to be loyal Communists who would serve Mother Russia. Many would be arrested. Some simply disappeared.

Several thousand men would remain and settle in Italy. Most of them stayed because they married local women. The majority of the men would be taken to England.

Even Wojtek moved to England with his troops. Actually his unit was stationed in the village of Hutton in Scotland. When his unit was demobilized, Wojtek was donated to the Edinburgh Zoo. Soldiers whom he would recognize when they spoke Polish to him would continue to visit him.

I had to wrestle with my decision. I had met a woman and wanted to remain in Italy. But my entire family was now in England and I also wanted to be with them. In the end I decided to stay with family.

Once they had arrived in England, Bolek and Dolek and the other Polish cadets were officially admitted to the Royal Air Force and attended the RAF Technical School. The Polish students were behind their classmates because the British students had already graduated high school. Bolek and Dolek had just finished grade 5 but they kept up.

These were the first 'foreigners' ever to go to that school which was the largest air force school in England. So there was a problem when Christmas holidays were nearing. The school would be closed for the holidays and the students would all go home. The Polish children had no place to go so the camp officers put an ad in the local newspaper asking if British families would take these children in for the holidays. There were at this time 300 young Polish cadets in England.

The response was overwhelming with over 600 invitations. The Countess of Jersey requested two young boys. As Dolek and Bolek were identical twins, they were selected to visit the Countess and her family at Richmond Palace. At the last minute, when Bolek realized that they would be staying with a Countess, he chickened out and another boy took his place. The Countess took to Dolek right away and a very special bond quickly formed between the two. Soon, Virginia decided that she wanted to meet Bolek. As she was very accustomed to getting what she wanted, she called her driver and off they went to pick up Bolek from the place that he was staying. From that time on, the boys spent all of their vacations with The Earl and Countess of Jersey, and their family. After several years, Virginia wrote to our mother requesting permission to formally adopt both Dolek and Bolek. The adoption process was three months away from completion when the marriage of Virginia and the Earl of Jersey started to fall apart. Regardless of a formal adoption, Virginia and the boys would remain close for the rest of her life. She would take our entire family all under her wings and became Aunt Virginia to all of us.

When I arrived in England, I was put into a school to learn English. I was going to continue my job as liaison official between our forces and the British army. But this time it meant that I had to learn how to do paperwork, a lot of paperwork. This wasn't the type of work I wanted to do. So I went back to school to get an agricultural degree.

The Polish army, in England, was dissolving so I had to decide what to do. I had several choices. I could settle in England. An aunt who lived in Baltimore, Maryland had contacted us. She wanted to sponsor us to move to America. Our new aunt Virginia invited us all to visit with her, so that she could discuss her plans as well. Virginia suggested that we should move to Canada. She offered to assist the family with a loan to purchase a farm, so that the entire family could relocate together. Virginia was already planning to move back to the United States. She suggested that by moving to Canada, she would be able to then help the family get the proper papers for everybody to move to the U.S.

There was one major reason why I would choose Canada. Canada was looking for immigrants from England. You could even buy a farm while still in England. Which is what I wanted to do. In the book listing Canadian farms for sale, I found a farm that I liked in southern Ontario. I gathered my money and with the loan from aunt Virginia, we now owned a farm in Canada.

There was just one minor problem. I had 410 British pounds but I would only be allowed to take 200 pounds out of England. Which is when a British officer showed me how these things were done. He took me to a branch of the Canadian Royal Bank in London. I deposited my money and it was transferred into a bank in Toronto.

On April 28, 1948 I stepped off the boat in Halifax where an agent of the Canadian Pacific Railway met me. Just off the boat, a young girl came up to me, probably because I was still wearing my army uniform. She had a basket of apples and asked that I take one.

"Which one?" I asked. And she picked out the biggest apple in the basket and gave it to me.

Such was my welcome to Canada.

The agent took me to the railway station and put me onto a train heading to Montreal. It would be a 2-day trip, I was told. And I was put into a first class car. A porter showed me to a sleeping car with a bed and new pajamas just waiting for me.

"Just change into these and give me your clothes," the porter told me.

I did, as he said not knowing what would happen to my clothes. The next morning the same porter gently woke me from a good sleep. He had my clothes cleaned and my shoes shined, and then he had breakfast brought to me. I could get used to this kind of train travel.

In Montreal, I was met by another Canadian Pacific Railway agent who put me onto a train to Toronto. In Toronto I would meet the government agent who would take me to my new land.

At the government office, I found out that the farm I thought I had bought had been sold two years previously. They wanted me to hire myself out as a farmhand but I would have nothing to do with it. I had been promised a farm and I was going to own it, one way or another.

But there was also some good news. I went to the Royal Bank in Toronto expecting to get about $1,650 Canadian with a little bit of interest thrown in. What a surprise when I found over $3,400 in my account.

During the entire time I was with the British army they were taking a bit of money from what I was being paid. When I deposited my money into the bank and transferred it to Canada, the army matched my deposit.

I had enough for a deposit for a farm. Now I just had to find one.

They found a Polish-speaking real estate agent in the Niagara Peninsula. He showed me several farms that simply weren't worth trying to farm. Finally he brought me to see a farm in Wellandport. The house was old but it was livable. The barn was run down (run down to the point that my first cow ran through the wall to get outside) but could be fixed. An older couple named the Collvers owned it. Mrs. Collver was the first to know that this is where I was going to settle. She told her husband that he was going to sell me the farm.

Once I was settled, Eddie, Dolek and Bolek came and joined me on the farm. Months later, our mother, sisters and our new brother-in-law, Joe Jablecki, Sophie's husband would all join us. Per the instructions of Virginia's loan, the farm was held in the names of the four men in the family. Farming was not an easy life, and the others had different plans for their lives. Eddie found work at a foundry and purchased the first car in the family, a 1935 Dodge. Soon he would marry and buy a home in Welland, signing off on his portion of the farm. Dolek and Bolek would also get jobs at General Motors and they also moved away from the farm, signing off on their portion of the farm. Sophie and Joe would settle in St. Catherines. Loni married and also settled in Welland.

Years later, as promised by aunt Virginia, immigration papers for the U.S. arrived. Dolek and Bolek accepted her invitation and both left Canada for a new life in California.

I married and stayed on the farm in Wellandport, the best place I could ever imagine in which to live.

Conclusion

Franklin Roosevelt seemed to know that America would eventually be drawn into the war. And he knew that Germany had to be beaten. America would attack Germany before they went after Japan.

It was in August 1941; months before the Americans entered the war, when Roosevelt and Churchill met in secret off the coast of Newfoundland. There, they drew up the Atlantic Charter that established what Europe would look like after the war. One of its main points was that all pre-war borders were to be respected; were to be put back as they were before Hitler's and Stalin's invasions. It was also agreed that Stalin would have to agree to this Charter if he wanted to receive Allied help against Hitler's invading armies.

Stalin agreed in public. But, in private, he demanded a secret agreement allowing him to keep the lands of Poland, Finland and the

Baltic States that Hitler had given him.

Churchill was furious. It was British arms that were keeping Russia from being over-run by Germany. But Stalin had an ally in Anthony Eden. After condemning Chamberlain's policy of appeasement with Hitler, he was ready to give over the lives of tens of millions of people to appease Stalin.

Roosevelt probably didn't know much about Stalin or life in the Soviet Union. When the Soviets began to fight Hitler, Roosevelt idealized Stalin. Roosevelt believed that Stalin would succumb to his American charm and tried to keep Churchill out of these negotiations. Eventually, neither of these allied leaders would have the backbone to stand up to Stalin.

Stalin, who had no real leverage, walked away with everything he wanted. The three leaders had made the Soviet Union a future superpower.

One minor problem remained. Britain and America were democracies and most of their citizens were still appalled at the war started by Hitler and Stalin. Churchill and Roosevelt called in their media friends for help. They needed to make Stalin into a hero and the Soviet Union into the savior of the free world.

Lord Beaverbrook, who owned a newspaper empire including the Daily Express, was already calling for public support for the Soviets. He now went into overdrive. Many Britains, who had adopted Polish airmen, now abandoned them.

In the US, papers and magazines told the stories of the heaven, created by Stalin, which was in danger of being destroyed by the Germans. Hollywood joined in by making movies about the struggle of the Russian people who had been attacked without provocation. Or so the movies said.

The whole world had to come to the aid of the Soviet Union and had to give Stalin anything he desired.

When word of the atrocities committed by the Soviets came to light, they were ignored. When the bodies of thousands of Polish officers, who had been murdered by the Soviets, were discovered in the Katyn Forest it was the Poles who were accused of being troublemakers because they wanted to uncover the truth. When the Polish Home Army in Warsaw arose to throw out the Nazis, they received little help from their allies. The Russians waited, just outside Warsaw, watching the Germans massacre its citizens.

In the battle, early in the war, to keep Warsaw free and in this battle to regain its freedom more Poles were killed than there were Americans killed in all the battles of the entire war. Yet the media remained silent.

Churchill professed to be Poland's ally. But he didn't have the courage to stand up to Stalin.

Roosevelt was already preparing for a new world order after the war. He considered countries such as France, Germany, Poland and the Baltic nations as being 'old Europe'. They were to be ignored. Britain and the

Soviet Union were 'new Europe'. They had to be strengthened. These two nations, along with the United States and China, would, after the war, control the politics of the entire world. These four nations would be the only ones that would be allowed to maintain an army. They wouldn't allow any other nation to develop into a power that could threaten them. And the United States would be the major power. This would bring peace to the world. At least that is what Roosevelt thought.

When the war was over, a victory parade was held in London where all the Allied nations were to be represented. Even if that nation had not sent any troops their flag would be in the parade. Only one nation was to be excluded. Poland provided the fourth largest army to the Allied cause. And that is only if you consider the Soviet Union working for the Allied cause. But Stalin insisted that no Polish troops or flags be allowed in the celebration.

The history of war is written by the winners, by the people in power. When Churchill wrote about the war, he seemed to forget that his policies were largely responsible for the power of Stalin and the onset of the cold war.

American history glosses over Roosevelt's part in establishing the conditions for cold war. He seemed to trust 'Uncle Joe' when he was negotiating the terms for peace once the war would end. The Americans kept trusting the Soviets after Roosevelt's death. After America dropped its nuclear weapons on Japan, Stalin finally declared war on Japan. The

Japanese, in China, surrendered to the Soviets. Their weapons were given to the Chinese Communists. This, in turn, led to the Communists taking China from its American friends.

Newspapers and magazines fell in line against the Communists when the cold war was declared. Hollywood destroyed most of their pro Soviet movies. Others were edited to remove the pro Soviet propaganda and leave only the war scenes. Some of these movies are being restored. Two of these restored movies, both originally filmed in 1943, were recently played on satellite T.V.

The first was "The North Star" starring Anne Baxter, Dana Andrews and Walter Huston with producer Samuel Goldwyn.

The second was "Mission To Moscow" from Warner Brothers' starring Walter Huston, Ann Harding and Oscar Homolka.

Between the two movies, a commentator did explain the history of these movies.

Just as a sidebar. I could never understand why so many Americans and British betrayed their countries to give military and political secrets to the Soviets. Not until I discovered this part of history, a part that few people want to know about.

The majority of Americans and British believed the propaganda that was being put out during the Second World War. They believed that the Soviets were the victims of a world conspiracy against them.

Most of the people, eventually, realized how wrong they were. But thousands never did. Hundreds, who worked for their governments in security and research, still felt that it was their duty to help their comrades.

Such is the power of the media.

Appendix

Here are a few books that may enhance this story:

Poland 1939: The Birth of Blitzkrieg
(Osprey Campaign) by Steven J. Zaloga

A Question Of Honor. The Kosciuszko Squadron. Forgotten Heroes Of World War 11
by Lynne Olson and Stanley Cloud

Stolen Childhood. A Saga Of Polish War Children
by Lucjan Krolikowski

Rising '44: The Battle for Warsaw
by Norman Davies

The Uprooted
by William B. Makowski

No Greater Ally: The Untold Story of Poland's Forces in World War II
by Kenneth Koskodan

The Long Walk: The True Story of a Trek to Freedom
by Slavomir Rawicz

Without Vodka: Adventures in Wartime Russia
by Aleksander Topolski

Gulag: A History
by Anne Applebaum

The following web site catalogs the names of "Victims of Soviet Repression". It lists the names of people who were exiled: http://www.indeks.karta.org.pl/en/index.html

When checking for our family, for men check under the surname Dobrucki and for women check under the surname Dobrucka.

www.ingramcontent.com/pod-product-compliance
Lightning Source LLC
Chambersburg PA
CBHW061657040426
42446CB00010B/1791